THE GUN DIGEST® BOOK OF
Shotgunning

MARTY FISCHER

©2010 Krause Publications, Inc.,
a subsidiary of F+W Media, Inc.

Published by

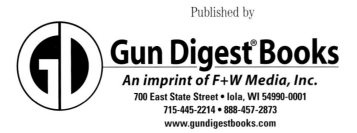

Gun Digest® Books

An imprint of F+W Media, Inc.
700 East State Street • Iola, WI 54990-0001
715-445-2214 • 888-457-2873
www.gundigestbooks.com

Our toll-free number to place an order or obtain
a free catalog is (800) 258-0929.

Cover photo courtesy of M.D. and Julia Johnson, M & J Outdoor Communications

Library of Congress Control Number: 2009937525

ISBN 13: 978-1-4402-1111-9
ISBN 10: 1-4402-1111-6

Designed by Dave Hauser

Edited by Corrina Peterson

Printed in China

TABLE OF CONTENTS

FOREWORD

I cannot remember the dog's name, but I do recollect that he was a beautiful black and white Springer spaniel. I can, however, remember with vivid detail every minute of the hunt. The morning sky overhead was a beautiful turquoise blue, and the cottonwood trees along the creek bottom were in their vivid fall colors of red, gold and yellow. It was as perfect a day as any outdoorsmen could wish for.

As we moved quietly through the grass, the Springer hit the scent of a bird and started quartering back and forth to hone in on the bird moving in front of him. Fortunately the little dog was well trained, so he stayed less than 25 yards from us as he worked the bird.

He went about his business quickly, looping left or right at the end of each pass and jumping up from the tall grass to see where we were. We followed him for another 50 or so yards before his demeanor changed from excited to dead serious as he locked in on the bird.

We both knew what was coming, and we were ready. The little dog made one last check on our location before bursting full speed forward to flush the bird. A beautiful cock pheasant came up fast, clawing the air with its large wings and cackling as he gained speed and altitude. The bird was on a left to right course that took him away from me, but it would offer my hunting partner a 30-yard shot. This bird was on a course that, over the years to come, I would learn was sudden death to any bird that Marty Fischer wished to put in his bag.

That was the first time I hunted with Marty, and that perfect fall day would be the first of many hunts he and I would enjoy in the years to come. We found that we had many things in common. It turns out that we were both natives of the Deep South, and we both had a long family tradition of hunting. We both had a passion for shotgunning and we made our living in the outdoors industry.

I met Marty in Cody, Wyoming, when he was a segment host on the well-known TV series, Suzuki Great Outdoors on ESPN. He wrote shotgun and wingshooting articles for many outdoor magazines that I enjoyed reading. My son Richard and I owned a company that produced instructional shotgun videos called Sunrise Productions.

Marty and I quickly became friends and we started exploring ways that we could combine our efforts. We made a few bird hunting videos and one on sporting clays. We produced a pilot for a TV show, and the Shotgun Journal television series was born.

The videos and the Shotgun Journal gave us a chance to hunt birds all over the world. We made numerous trips to Argentina for pigeons, doves, ducks, geese and perdiz. We chased francolin, guinea fowl, doves, pigeons, ducks and geese in Africa, red-legged partridge in Spain, pheasants in Hungary and pretty much every huntable bird species in North America. Over the years we have spent hundreds of hours talking about shotguns, different shooting methods and comparing every species of bird we have hunted and the ones we would like to hunt.

Hosting the show and producing wingshooting videos and DVDs has allowed me to hunt with some of the best shotgunners in the world, and I can say with no reluctance that Marty Fischer is the best natural wingshooter I have ever encountered.

Over the years he has gained a good reputation as a sporting clays course designer, and is sought after as a sporting clays and wingshooting coach. I can only attest to two character flaws in this otherwise fine man. First, he is reluctant to shoot a side by side shotgun; a true gentleman's gun. The second flaw is the one that I find most disturbing. In recent years he has taken up with a bad crowd and has started to hunt the wild turkey. I simply cannot understand why one of the best wingshooters in the world would get up before dawn just to shoot at a bird standing still less than 40 yards away.

Enjoy the read. It will make you a better shot.

Bruce Scott
Sunrise Productions

Given our long history, I can confidently say that I have probably spent more time in the field and blind with Marty than any other person. I have watched him shoot thousands of birds over the years. I am very qualified to tell you that if you read the following pages with any degree of attention, your shotgunning skills on birds and/or clays will most certainly improve.

INTRODUCTION

In a perfect world, wingshooters who venture afield with shotgun in hand in search of elusive gamebirds would wish to have complete mastery over their brain, their hands and their eyes. With such control they could precisely steer a scattergun's muzzle in the direction of their quarry to take shots that would never be missed. In other words, they would experience wingshooting utopia shot after shot. Impossible you say? Not necessarily. In the perfect wingshooter's world, this remarkable feat of never missing is actually attainable.

There are, however, many variables in wingshooting that can contribute to hits and misses, so the individual being has thus far been unable to consistently attain the perfection he seeks. The act of hitting a flying object, whether it be feathered or clay, with a shot charge propelled hundreds of miles per hour through the air is truly an art. Successful shooting requires a unique combination of eye and hand coordination, fueled by a split second visual and mental dissemination of information to determine the target's identification, speed, angle and distance. It is the vast variety of possible target presentations that make wingshooting one of the ultimate mental and physical challenges known to man. And it is this challenge that has stimulated me to write *The Gun Digest Book of Shotgunning*.

For generations, sportsmen have ventured afield to face the winged challenge of gamebird species found throughout the world. These target types come in a variety of shapes, sizes and speeds. As a result, they offer the hunter a wide array of flight patterns, which are presented at different speeds, angles and distances. The smallest gamebird weighs just a few ounces, and the largest can tip the scales at more than 20 pounds. And if that's not enough, throw in the uncanny ability of some game birds to unpredictably maneuver in flight and you can see why shooting sportsmen constantly seek a more efficient means of attaining consistency in the field.

Over the years, innovations such as interchangeable shotgun chokes, smokeless powder and adjustable stocks have made it somewhat easier for the hunter to cope with the eccentricities of wingshooting. But with all of the creative powers of the human mind, no invention has proven to be fool-proof when it comes to a shooter's success or failure. In virtually every case, and with every innovation known to wingshooting in place, the difference between hits and misses rests solely on the shooter's ability to put the physical and mental pieces of the shooting puzzle together within a time frame measured in fractions of a second. *The Gun Digest Book of Shotgunning* is written to deal with live birds, so each shooting scenario discussed will most likely result in a totally new puzzle for the shooter to solve.

Without question, an accomplished gun can visually and mentally absorb all of the information needed for a successful shot once he locks focus on a bird. This ability allows him to perform a series of mechanical and technical movements which place the muzzle of the shotgun in a position to sufficiently move the gun ahead of the target's line of flight in order to deliver a shot charge onto that target. While a great deal of this effort can be described as instinctive, good wingshooting skills can be developed through proper instruction and practice, which in turn will create the positive habits required for the mechanical, technical and mental aspects of the sport. Competent instruction, followed by those hours of practice, can help transform even the newest of shooters into skilled wingshooters.

Unfortunately, with limits and seasons being what they are throughout most of the shooting world, the field is really not the best place to practice. Wingshooting skills are more easily developed through the various clay target games such as trap, skeet and sporting clays. Of the three, sporting clays is certainly the most realistic to actual hunting, but any shooting practice is certainly better than none.

The Gun Digest Book of Shotgunning is about the mechanics and techniques of shotgun shooting that can be learned and developed over time. It has been said that no shooter anywhere in the world is the same. All of them have different physical and visual skills, and they see lead pictures differently. The information provided in this book is not necessarily new or innovative. It is simply a compilation of important 'how to' information that is available to the wingshooting enthusiast.

I suggest that as you read this book you make the information discussed herein a part of your own personal practice. If you are so inclined, spend some time with a competent professional shooting instructor. Chances are he can provide you with specific modifications or changes to your mechanics or technique that will provide immediate help.

Best of luck with your shooting, and I hope you enjoy *The Gun Digest Book of Shotgunning*.

Marty Fischer
Rincon, Georgia

The Basics
of Wingshooting

Let's face it. In order for a wingshooter to become competent in the field, he must have the basics of shooting flying objects firmly in place. Wingshooting is an eye/hand coordination game. The eyes see the target and send information about the target to the brain. The brain then signals the finger to pull the trigger once the desired lead picture is confirmed. This process sounds easy, and it is when the pieces of the puzzle fall into place. So let's get right to those pieces of the puzzle.

Once a shooter learns to use his vision to see the target, he must have a working knowledge and understanding of the physical movement required to place the muzzle of his shotgun in a location relative to that moving target. When the muzzle of the gun is pushed to the right spot, the pellets from the fired shotshell will impact the intended target. He must take into consideration that he is sending a speeding shot charge traveling somewhere in the neighborhood of 800 miles per hour in the direction of a moving target traveling at a much slower pace. The very best shooters seem to have a knack for deciphering information that includes target speed, angle and distance so as to allow their eyes and hands work as a team in placing the shotgun muzzle in just that right spot relative to the target as the trigger is pulled. The not so skilled or trained, however, can visibly struggle with the same challenge.

A major secret to a shooter's success is having excellent technique. A good stance, proper balance and a perfect gun mount are keys to consistent success.

Shooting a shotgun can be as easy as pointing your finger. Since a shotgun is pointed and not aimed, the ability to focus on an object and point at it is the first step towards wingshooting success.

It is true that some members of the species *homo sapien* have inherently better physical and visual skills to draw from. These individuals tend to be the so-called "natural" shots that you might hear about from time to time. This natural ability is merely a superior blend of eye/hand coordination that one might find in professional athletes such as baseball or tennis players. In fact, most professional athletes make excellent wingshooters because of their ability to let their eyes lead their hands to a successful end. Great vision and superb reflexes allow those natural shots to see and react to moving objects in a totally different way than does the average shooter.

Since most shooters don't have the aforementioned tremendous natural ability, it is comforting to know that wingshooting skills can be learned and subsequently developed through proper training and practice. Like most top athletes in other

Most shooters got their start by shooting a .22 caliber rifle. With open sights, the rifle is aimed at a specific target. Shooting a shotgun in the field is quite different.

If possible, it's best to shoot a shotgun with both eyes open. You are much better off using 100% of your visual capacity instead of closing an eye, which limits depth perception and peripheral skills.

sports, the best shooters constantly hone their skills by taking quality instruction and practicing continuously. This book is written to provide concise information that, when applied properly, can open a number of doors that lead to significant improvement of one's wingshooting skills. The most effective way to do this is to break a successful shot down to its most basic elements.

First of all, shooting a shotgun is much like pointing your finger. You will find that by simply focusing on an object and then pointing at it with either hand, chances are pretty good that you will never miss that object with your finger. This will be the case whether the chosen target is station-

ary or moving. Give it a try. Pick out an object and point at it while keeping both eyes open. Remember to point and not aim. Right on, I'll bet. So if you can successfully allow the eyes to lead the hands to an object without a shotgun in them, chances are you can do the same thing with a shotgun in hand.

Keep in mind that wingshooting is quite different from shooting a stationary object with a rifle or a pistol. Those types of firearms have both front and rear sights that must be properly aligned on a target in order to hit it with a single projectile. Since this alignment must be very precise, hitting a moving object like a speedy game bird with

Successful shooting starts with a good stance, which allows the body to move freely throughout the shot sequence.

either of them would be very difficult.

A shotgun is a different animal all together. Since there is no rear sight on the models used for shooting flying objects like gamebirds and clay targets, the gun is pointed and not aimed. When you consider the absence of a rear sight, you'll find that the shooter's eye on the side of the shooting shoulder takes its place. Assuming the gun fits the shooter properly and is mounted to the face and placed in the shoulder correctly, the gun should shoot exactly where the shooter is looking.

Since the gun will shoot to the point of the

shooter's focus when properly fitted and mounted, he should always look down the rib or through the beads of the gun and directly on the target itself or to a point ahead of the target depending on his shooting style. If at any time the eyes leave that focal point relative to the target and are directed back to the barrel for shooter alignment, or they look at some object other than the intended target, the result will almost always be a miss.

The shooter's ability to use his eyes to acquire a lead picture is not the only ingredient needed for a successful shot. Things like proper foot and body position and a well executed gun mount are also required if a shot is to be successful. These important elements of successful shooting require physical motion and can be learned and applied with proper practice.

At first, mastering the basics of wingshooting might appear to be difficult for some new shooters, as the thought of having to determine just what sight picture is needed to hit a constantly moving and changing flying target can be confusing. Even though humans are not blessed with the best vision in nature, they do have a mental capacity that is superior to all creatures. As a result, we can see and feel lead pictures that can in fact be learned and stored mentally for future use. You will find that shotgun leads are not measured. On shots taken in the field, there simply isn't time.

Professional instructors often tell their students to feel the lead, not measure it. The eyes will tell the shooter when the picture is right. Without question,

The more crossing a target is to your position, the more lead you will need to hit it. Don't be afraid to miss in front of those crossing birds.

Good technique includes a precise insertion point to complement the shooting style you plan to use on a given shot.

As the muzzle is inserted relative to the bird, the hands start to move to the desired lead. Your head should stay planted in the gun.

Once the shot is taken, the shooter can transfer the eyes to a second target.

the more information that is stored for immediate recall when a bird is flushed or passes overhead, the more instinctively the shooter will respond. As this skill is further developed, the shooter's ability to feel the lead will become more natural.

A good understanding of how the eyes and brain work together to direct the hands can give a shooter a leg up when it comes to his shooting skills. These skills can only be developed with proper practice. Like other physical skills that require precise use of the motor movement senses, the proper and controlled mechanics for handling a shotgun have to be learned and developed to the point that they become habitual or as some might say, instinctive.

Being an accomplished shot with a shotgun doesn't bear any resemblance to passing a college course in rocket science, but many shooters seem to take it to that level. Once the basic motor skills of mounting and swinging a shotgun are mastered, and a series of mental images of lead pictures for certain shots are filed away in the brain, lead picture identification becomes more natural. And when all of the elements needed for a successful shot are in place, the shooter will be amazed at how natural it feels when a target such as a pheasant or duck presents itself in front of the gun. The eyes will lock on the target and the hands will masterfully push the gun towards the bird. As this sequence of events unfolds, everything to the shooter seems to be in slow motion. Remarkably the eyes and brain instinctively know when the proper sight picture is acquired and, as the shot sequence continues, the shooter will see the bird fall while focusing on it through the beads on the gun.

Did the shooter have the time to decipher all of the aspects of the shot in the few seconds it took for this scene to play out? If he was successful, chances are he would say that the gun just went to the right spot and the trigger was pulled when the muzzle got to the target and the picture felt right. Many would define this action as instinctive, but once we analyze how the sequence of events unfolded, instinct might be only a small part of what actually happened. It might be better to say that the satisfying result of such a shot sequence was a combination of the eyes, hands and brain working as a team. You will find that as you become more comfortable with your wingshooting it is this teamwork of senses and our remarkable mind that ultimately define the basics of wingshooting.

Since there is much more to the above scenario than just pointing the gun until it feels good, let's take a look at the myriad of variables that allow such a shot to take place.

Selecting
the Right Gun

The wingshooting opportunities found throughout the world are quite diverse, as there are many species of game birds for hunters to pursue. This is especially true in North America, where millions of hunters annually venture afield in search of game birds from ducks and geese to dove, quail, pheasants, partridge, woodcock and grouse. This diversity of bird types can present problems when a hunter is faced with a decision regarding the type of shotgun he wants to use. As much as they would like to buy a new shotgun for every species they hunt, most wingshooters tend to look for one gun that can handle a majority of their shooting needs. The debate on shotgun choice will go on as long as two or more hunters can find birds to pursue, but in most cases, their choices are usually narrowed down between 12 or 20 gauge models. The main reason for this is that a wide variety of loads are available for those two gauges. These loads possess adequate knockdown power to handle virtually any game bird on the planet when used in the proper place. As a result, most shooters make the choice for their primary wingshooting gun between these two gauges.

There are, of course, other shotgun gauges that have been popular among wingshooters for decades, but due to either high ammunition costs, limited manufacturing quantities or a lack of knockdown power, they enjoy only specialized use today. As one might expect, there are purists who will always swear by their favorite 16, 28 or .410 gauge scattergun. At the same time, the huge 10 gauge chambered for up to 3 ½-inch loads seems to rise and fall in popularity depending on legal shot types and limits on turkeys or waterfowl, the species for which it is mostly used. In recent years, the three and a half inch 12 gauge has been introduced, and has taken the place of the mighty 10 bore in many gun cabinets.

Of these gauges, the 28 is considered by many experts to be superior in terms of overall patterning and performance. For some reason, the .550 bore of the 28 gauge delivers a dense center core of pellet hits on pattern boards throughout the range of its chokes. As a result of its superior patterning characteristics, this gauge is deadly on

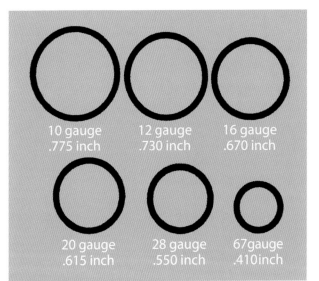

When it comes to shotgunning, selecting the right gauge to get the job done is important. This illustration represents the actual bore size of the different gauges. The gauge is determined by the number of lead balls of the size listed it would take to equal one pound. The .410 is not listed by gauge, but by bore size. It is actually a 67 gauge.

Many wingshooters prefer a quick pointing small gauge gun for upland shooting.

small upland gamebirds.

The little 28 is very popular with quail and woodcock hunters, but it is generally considered a bit light for larger wild gamebirds such as pheasants and some species of grouse. The 28 has never been considered a waterfowl gauge, and with today's non-toxic shot restrictions, it probably never will be. Using steel loads with the 28 would not be practical for all but the smallest of gamebirds, but some of the newer non-toxic, non-steel loads are available in 28 gauge, making it an option for close in decoy or timber shooting for ducks. Bismuth and soft tungsten-based loads have proven quite effective in these hunting situations.

The 16 gauge fell prey to the 12 gauge/ 20 gauge marketing push put on by gun and ammunition manufacturers, as it was considered too similar to those two gauges to warrant extensive manufacture after the 1970's. Sadly, many wingshooters will never get to experience the feel of a well made 16 bore, even though some gun makers introduce models to their product lines from time to time.

Many parents start their youngsters on a .410

gauge, primarily because of the absence of recoil. Unfortunately they don't realize that the .410 is the most difficult of all gauges to shoot consistently. The fact that there are fewer pellets in any .410 load than in any other gauge means that at best shooters are looking at very sparse, narrow patterns. The smallness of the bore is only capable of producing a long shot string and a fairly narrow pattern which makes this gauge more suited for the advanced shooter rather than the beginner.

Gauge versus bore

The .410 is the only gauge that really isn't a gauge. The .410 is instead the bore diameter of the barrel. The others are gauges, which means that the gauge number is the number of lead balls the size of the bore diameter needed to weigh one pound. So 12 lead balls measuring .729 inches would weigh one pound when weighed.

This little gauge is fine for stationary targets out to around 30 yards away, but for fast flying wild birds it's better left in very skilled hands.

New shooters would be better suited to start with a 28 or 20 gauge gun using the lightest loads available. For more mature novice shooters, a 12 gauge using either 7/8 ounce training loads or low velocity one ounce loads will be ideal. Once the shooter gets accustomed to his gun and is comfortable with its recoil, he can move to heavier loads that suit the type of target he will be shooting or whatever bird he will be hunting. Getting turned off to shooting early in the game because of poor gun or ammo choice won't do much to keep a shooter interested in the sport. It is far better to learn how to shoot comfortably away from the field than it is to get your teeth kicked in by an overpowering load.

SHOTGUN ACTION TYPES

For many years there have been four popular types of shotgun actions used for wingshooting. They are the side by side or double barrel, over and under, the semi-automatic and the pump action. All of these actions are appropriate for just about any gamebird, and which action the shooter chooses to use is purely a matter of personal choice. Let's take a closer look at each of them and how they are applicable to the various types of wingshooting.

SIDE BY SIDE SHOTGUNS

When it comes to wingshooting, no shotgun action possesses more charm, character and history than the side by side. For hundreds of years this double gun has been the standard by which all other scatterguns were judged. And with such great names as Purdey, Holland and Holland, Fox, Lefever, Winchester, Parker and L.C. Smith, the rich tradition associated with bird hunting

Double guns come in many models, grades, barrel lengths and gauges. These are representative of some of the best guns of all time: (l to r) W.C. Scott 8-gauge made in 1878, Parker VH 12 gauge made in 1928, L.C. Smith .410 made in 1921, Arrieta 578 12 gauge and Arrieta 578 28 gauge.

Many side by side shooters are as interested in the tradition of the guns as they are about shooting them.

was founded with the double barrel shotgun as its benchmark. It is comforting to note that this tradition lives on today, even though the everyday demand for side by side shotguns has dwindled significantly over the past few decades.

Unfortunately, a large number of the side by side shotguns in the hands of hunters today have been passed down over the years from father to son, and are merely conversation pieces rather than useful field pieces. In most cases, the double guns being produced today tend to be a bit pricey, and a large percentage of hunters simply cannot afford a quality piece, even if they wanted one. But for those shooters who can afford a well made side by side, they will have a gun that is both a joy to shoot and an excellent investment as well.

The side by side craze these days tends to be for guns in the smaller gauges. In many circles, it's the 20 and 28 gauge guns that command the bulk of the attention when it comes to the side by side action. There are still 10 and 12 gauge models be-

ing produced, but a sizable number of side by side purchasers these days are upland bird enthusiasts who love the tradition of hunting with a small bore scattergun.

Many doubles come with the straight English stocks, which were developed primarily for shooting flushing or driven birds. And keeping with tradition, it's the double gun that is still the standard bearer even today in Europe, where most of the bird shooting is of the flushing or driven variety.

For years American waterfowlers used long barreled double guns with different chokes in each barrel. One of the barrels was usually choked for shots on birds that were in close to medium range, and one for birds at distance. It's this option that helped make the double gun so popular. The die-hard waterfowlers often wanted their barrels long and their chokes tight and tighter. They relished being able to harvest ducks and geese at ranges that would be considered long, even by today's standard.

Sadly, the double barrel really never caught on with clay target shooters, probably because they were looking for a narrower sight plane to consistently acquire the precise lead pictures required in games like trap and skeet. Many shooters are typically interested in using what most other shooters use, so the popularity of other action types certainly played a role in the limited use of the side by side. In fact, the double barrel is probably the least popular action capable of holding two or more cartridges used by today's sportsmen. It will always, however, most likely be the most sought after action by collectors and purists due to the history and tradition that surrounds it.

OVER AND UNDER SHOTGUNS

The most popular double gun in use today for hunting and clay target shooting combined is the over and under. This action provides the shooter with a similar sight plane as is found on popular semi-automatic and pump models, but still offers the no nonsense, works every time reliability that wingshooters demand.

Additionally, the over and under can offer the shooter multiple choke options, so he can react to virtually any target presentation simply by selecting which barrel he plans to shoot first. This is especially effective in hunting situations, since different scenarios presented to the shooter will dictate whether he shoots the more open choke first or second.

As with the side by side, the over and under configuration is designed for both barrels to shoot to the same point of impact. As a result, the bottom barrel should typically carry the more open choke and should be shot first under normal situations. The laws of physics show that there is less stress on the shooter and gun if the lower of the two barrels is shot more often. This comment may raise some eyebrows, but physics are physics. You will note that on factory ported over and under

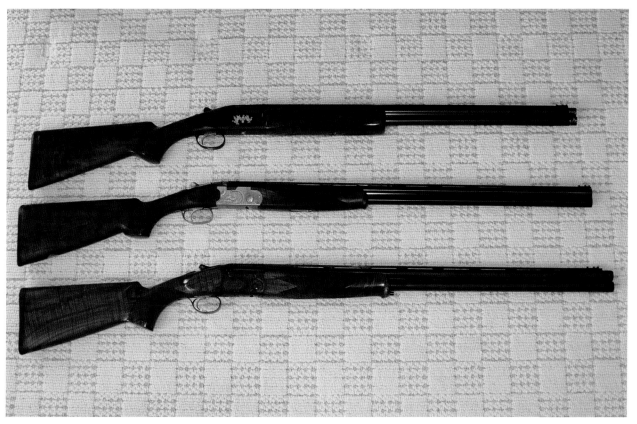

Many wingshooters, especially upland gunners, enjoy the feel of a fine over and under shotgun. Here are three of the most popular brands and models: (top to bottom) Browning Grade VI Citori 20 gauge, Beretta Silver Pigeon II 20 gauge, Caesar Guerini Summit 12 gauge.

Over and under shotguns come in a wide array of models, gauges, weights and barrel lengths.

models, the lower barrel often has more porting holes that does the top. This is an indication from the manufacturer that the lower barrel should be shot first under normal conditions.

In recent years the over and under has become the most popular action for clay target shooters, and with advent of sporting clays, a game which closely simulates actual hunting shots, virtually every gun company has developed a line of sporting clays models. These guns are specifically designed with more weight and a different balance point than the field grade models. Clay target models tend to be slightly heavier, and in most cases they are fitted with a wider "target acquisition" vent rib to help the shooter acquire his picture more quickly. With all of these positives for the wingshooter, one has to wonder why more hunters don't use the sporting clays models in the field.

For the most part double gun hunting models, whether side by side or over and under, tend to be lighter in weight than those designed for target shooting. It stands to reason that hunters don't relish lugging eight plus pound guns over hill and dale for six to eight hours in search of some feathered quarry, so models in the six and a half to seven pound range have been developed specifically for the field. Unfortunately shooters using these guns generally have to bear a bit more recoil, since the lighter weight usually results in more felt recoil. With limits being what they are, however, most hunters generally fire less than a dozen rounds on a hunt anyway, and as long as the gun fits properly, the lighter weight models should be comfortable to shoot. You will find, however, that the sporting configurations in the smaller gauges are perfect for the upland hunter, as the weight of those models tends to be significantly less than their 12 gauge counterparts.

Fortunately sporting clays guns have become so popular that some manufacturers have designed and marketed dual purpose models. These guns are built to possess the feel of a field gun, with the pointability of a clays gun. The weight and stock dimensions are set to complement the needs of the clay target shooter and the hunter. After all, today's clay target games are designed to simulate hunting, so guns that comfortably meet both needs seem to be a perfect fit.

The popularity of the over and under shotgun will almost certainly remain constant for years to come. Their reliability, flexibility and variety of price ranges make them among the best overall buys on the market today.

SEMI-AUTOMATIC ACTION SHOTGUNS

From John M. Browning's popular recoil operated semi-auto design of the early 20th century to the highly complex gas port ejection and rotating bolt guns of today, the semi-automatic shotgun has rapidly gained the favor of many wingshooters worldwide. Best known for the ability to rapidly fire its payload of shot shells with less felt recoil on the shooter, the semi-auto has become a fixture in the gun cases of bird hunters everywhere.

The advantages of the semi-automatic shotgun are easily documented. Perhaps the most common reason a person purchases this type of action is the recoil issue. The gas port system or inertia action which eject and chamber shells using the recoil generated when the gun is fired are both proficient at taking much of the felt recoil away from the shooter's face and shoulder. With other actions, the shoulder and face feel the full impact of the recoil generated when the gun is fired. Many manufacturers have added recoil suppressing parts in their actions to further reduce the felt recoil of the shot.

If there is a perceived disadvantage of the autoloader, it would be its reliability. Over the years many hunters have experienced troubles with the consistent cycling of their autoloader in the field. Some guns even required the shooter to reposition parts of the action in order to shoot light loads. Fortunately, most of the autoloaders made today are reputed to cycle the light loads and heavy loads interchangeably.

Because of the number of moving parts, the autoloader must be properly cleaned for it to cycle as it was designed to. Shooters will find that maintaining their autoloader after each hunt will insure consistent cycling the next time it goes to the field or range.

A second perceived advantage of the semi-auto is its ability to fire three or more shells before reloading. Many hunters see this as an advan-

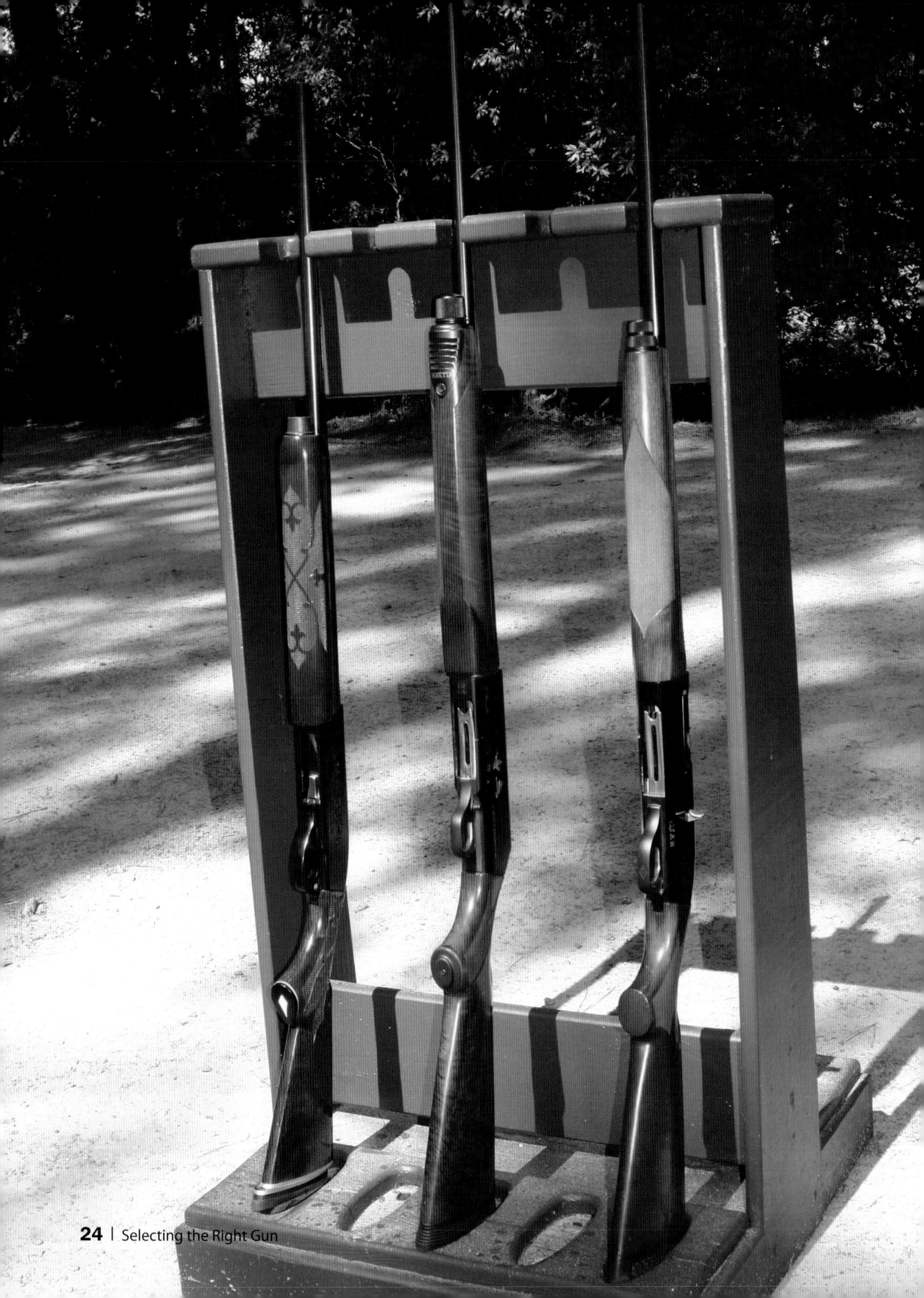

tage, but in reality, only the most skilled shooters can consistently make the third shot count, much less four or five when game laws allow that many shells to be loaded. In most cases, wild birds have reached a distance window that is beyond the skill level for the vast majority of shooters by the time the third shot is fired.

The choices of barrel length for semi-autos are varied, but most upland bird hunters choose 24 to 28-inch barrels, while waterfowlers tend to lean more toward longer barrels. Perhaps the reason for these choices is the need for a quick pointing piece for the lightning fast flushes of quail, grouse and woodcock in tight cover. On the other hand, many shots at waterfowl have traditionally been

Pictured at left are three of the most popular semiautomatic shotguns on the market. (l to r) Remington 1100 20 gauge and Beretta 390 12 gauge have gas operated systems. This Benelli Montefeltro (far right) has a left hand action and has an inertia operated system.

One of the most popular semiautomatic shotguns of all time is the Browning A-5. The Browning "humpback" set a standard for many years and was coveted by many American hunters. The A-5 features a recoil operated system, meaning that the recoil of the shot pushes the action and barrel backward to cycle another shell into the chamber.

at greater distances, and the sight plane of the longer barrel seems to provide better balance, a smoother swing and easier target acquisition.

Many hunters simply meet their needs by compromising with a 28-inch barrel, a choice that for years has been popular among the wingshooting fraternity using this type of action. Keep in mind, however, that with today's faster burning powders, barrel length will not affect shot shell performance, so the choice is merely one of personal preference. It should be noted that a 28 inch barrel on a semi-automatic shotgun will give the shooter about the same sight picture as he would see on a 30 inch barrel over and under or side by side. The length of the receiver on the auto is usually a couple of inches longer than on a double gun, so the sight plane between such models is slightly different.

Shooters should keep in mind that all semi-autos are not the same. There are inertia actions, recoil actions and gas system actions being offered by manufacturers around the world, and the felt recoil of the actions can be significantly different.

The gas operated gun features a gas port system that utilizes the gases generated when the powder ignites in a shot shell to enable the action of the gun. The dispersal of these gases and the movement of the gun's action means that the shooter feels less recoil. Keep in mind that the recoil is instant as the gun is being fired, but when you consider that the shot leaves the muzzle in mere fractions of a second, the felt recoil can be reduced.

Inertia action or recoil action semi autos have a completely different recoil feel than the gas guns. The inertia and recoil action models are operated by the recoil that is generated when a shell is fired. With the inertia system the bolt moves to load a second shell, while with the recoil action the barrel and bolt move to chamber additional shells. The felt recoil with the actions tend to be more violent than with a gas gun because more of the recoil with these actions is absorbed in the shooters face and shoulder.

Without question the most famous recoil action shotguns was the Browning A-5. This "humpback" model was a favorite of hunters for decades. When a shell was fired, the resulting recoil action within the gun moved the bolt back while loading another shell into the chamber. Today the Browning A-5 and a few other guns using the same action are still in use across the country.

PUMP ACTION SHOTGUNS

Many wingshooters will say that their favorite scattergun is one with a pump action. Unlike the

Waterfowlers tend to love a fine pump action shotgun, but they are quite functional for just about any gamebird. Here are three of the most popular pump shotgun models of all time: (top – Remington Wingmaster Magnum 20 gauge, middle – Browning BPS 20 gauge, bottom – Winchester Model 12 12 gauge).

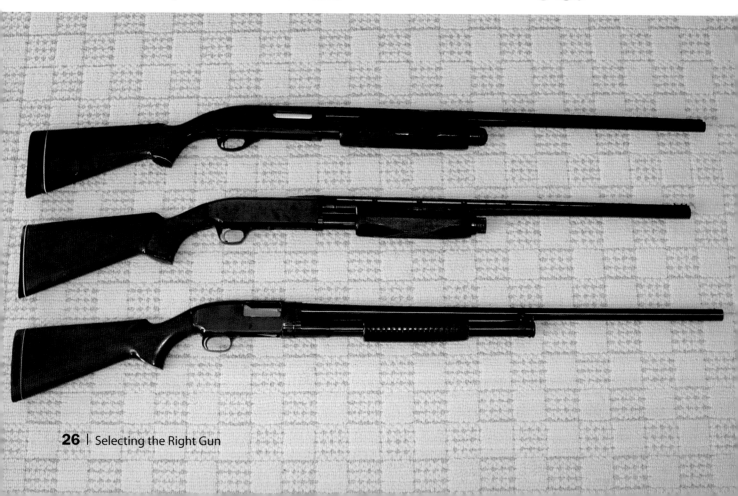

semi-automatic, the pump action is operated totally by the shooter. And, as with all actions, there are arguments for and against its use.

The pump action shotgun can help slow a shooter down since the gun will not fire until he has physically ejected and chambered another round. Many shooters claim that they can shoot a pump as fast as they can an auto, but why would they want too? Remember it's not how fast a gun will shoot that's important when it comes to wingshooting. It is more important for the shooter to stay within his physical and visual limitations and pull the trigger only when he sees what he feels is the right lead picture.

The pump has long been popular when climatic conditions might otherwise cause malfunctions with other action types due to cold or wet conditions. Since the action on a pump is operated by the shooter, it will usually function regardless of weather conditions.

Like the semi-automatic guns, pumps usually are designed to hold three or more shells. In wingshooting, however, it's hard to imagine that more than three shots could be taken in a single series of shots at birds in the field. Keep in mind, too, that most states limit chamber and magazine capacities to a maximum of three shells for bird hunting anyway, and federally mandated laws limit capacities to three rounds for all migratory bird hunting.

Pump action shotguns are not generally as heavy in weight as other types of actions, and recoil can be a problem, so keep that in mind when choosing target or hunting loads. If you are recoil sensitive, and choose to shoot a pump, gun fit becomes even more important.

The pump action shotgun as been around for decades, and chances are it will be constant addition to the gun cabinets of wingshooters for generations to come.

The type of shotgun action that you choose ultimately depends on your personal tastes. But whichever type you choose, always treat it as if it were loaded and remember to clean and maintain it properly. A properly maintained shotgun will last many lifetimes, and should be passed down from generation to generation.

Fitting a Gun for the Field

ost individuals who enjoy shotgun shooting just love to visit a gun shop where they can pick up various types and brands of shotguns to see how they feel in their hands. The same thing applies when visiting a shooting range. Invariably shooters want to get the feel of what the other guy is shooting. So with permission, they take a buddy's gun off the

While you can't shoot a gun at most firearms stores, you can get a feel for the balance and fit before making a purchase.

rack, check the action to make sure it is safe and put the gun to their face to get a mounted feel. What many shooters find amazing is how different one model feels from the next. Think about the times you've picked up a gun and brought it to your face and shoulder only to say "man, I could shoot that!"

Perhaps one of the more misunderstood aspects of wingshooting is proper gun fit. For years shooters have depended on old wives tales, myths and misinformation when the discussion of getting their guns fitted properly came up. Sadly for the most part, many shooters have been unknowingly shooting with guns that simply don't fit them correctly. The one size fits all philosophy simply doesn't apply to the shotgun industry.

What some shooters don't realize is that when they purchase a gun across the counter at their local gun stores, they are buying a gun designed to fit a person that conforms to a certain physical stature. Most mass produced guns are built to fit a shooter who stands about five feet, nine inches tall, with a 32 or 33 inch sleeve length and a medium build. Over the years, gunmakers found that by building their product to this standard, a majority of shooters could shoot their guns comfortably without major modifications. For the most part, that statement is true, but if your physical makeup varies somewhat from these measurements, chances are pretty good that your gun could use some modifications.

Surprisingly, a good percentage of shooters have fair success in the field despite the fact that they have fit themselves to the gun instead of the other way around. Just imagine how well they could shoot if the gun was fit properly so the eyes and the gun always looked at the same spot.

Good gun fit allows the shooter and gun to work as a team, because when the gun is properly fitted his visual focus will be only on the target or slightly ahead of it depending on the presentation. The visual focus will never be on the gun itself as sometimes happens with a poorly fitted shotgun. When the gun shoots where the eyes look, magical things can happen. A proper fit insures that the eyes can lead the hands and the gun to the correct lead picture and a successful shot.

Many shooters grew up thinking that proper gun fit was assured by placing the butt of the gun in the crook of the arm and matching the fleshy part of the index finger to the trigger. Unfortunately this measurement really has little to do with proper fit, since the arms are only a small part of the overall gun fit picture.

There are four major gun fit measurements that determine whether or not a shotgun fits a person

Gun fit can be a real issue, since not all shooters are shaped the same.

properly. They are length of pull, drop, cast and pitch. Let's take a look at the role that each of these measurements plays when it comes to the properly fitted gun.

LENGTH OF PULL

As discussed earlier, shooters have for years been measuring the gun in the crook of the arm to determine gun fit. When determining fit, this crook of the arm measurement could only have some affect on the length of the gun.

In addition to the arms, consideration must be given to the size of a persons hands, the thickness of his chest and shoulders, the length and width of his face, how much the shoulders slope and the length of the neck. It's these measurements in combination that precisely measure the correct length of pull.

There's something about a properly fitted shotgun that gives the shooter more confidence in the field. With a proper fit and mount, the gun will shoot exactly where the shooter looks. Well known outdoor writer Nick Sisley simply loves this Beretta DT-10.

There's an old wives' tale that says gun fit can be determined by putting the stock in the crook of the arm and matching up the finger to the trigger. Unfortunately there's a lot more to gun fit than this. It's an old wives tale, and it's just not true.

The length of pull for a shotgun is typically measured from the center of the trigger to the center of the butt plate. For years most American manufactured guns arrive from the factory with either 14 or 14 ¼ inch lengths of pull. Their European counterparts typically have 14 ½ or 14 ¾ inch length of pull. The fact is that stock lengths from 12 ½ to 16 inches will fit more than 90 percent of the shooters, so coming in somewhere in the middle is a good compromise for manufacturers of shotguns produced for the mass market.

A shooter should find a comfortable stock length that allows him to easily mount the gun to the face consistently without snagging the heel of the stock on his clothing. In most instances, a stock that is too long will cause it to be caught in the shooter's clothing as the mount is taking place.

With a stock that is too short, the shooter will find that the muzzle will dip noticeably as it is mounted. It is very important for the gun to mount cleanly and crisply, since any interruption in the muzzle coming to the line of the target could constitute a miss.

When the gun is properly mounted, one quick way to measure a good length of pull is to see a gap of 1 ½ to 2 ½ inches, typically two to three finger widths, between the shooter's nose and the base of the thumb on the trigger hand as it grips the gun. This is typically a good benchmark to work with. Keep in mind, however, that this holds true only if the gun is mounted properly and the

You can shoot a gun that's too long for you, but gun mounts will be a problem.

Guns that are too short for the shooter will often cause him to raise his head off the gun when shooting it, since an increase in felt recoil at the face could result.

The right length of pull makes a shotgun much easier to bring to the face and shoulder.

face is correctly placed on the comb of the gunstock.

Most of the time gunfitters will concentrate on fitting the gun for the comfort of the shooter. And when it comes to fitting the length of pull, they will tell you that a shooter should shoot the longest length of pull he is comfortable with. You'll find that you can shoot a gun that is a bit too long for you much better than you can one that is too short.

With most American field stocks, the drop from comb to heel is pretty steep, so the shooter needs to understand what the result of adding or subtracting length will be. By moving the face back or forward as a result of the adjustment, the vertical elevation of the master eye can be changed. This will have an affect on how the eye lines up down the rib, and is a determining factor on whether the gun shoots spot on, high or low.

It is important that the shooter be fitted in the clothing he intends to shoot in. Going from shooting in a T-shirt for early season doves to a heavy parka for late season waterfowl can drastically affect how comfortably the shooter can mount his gun. Some wingshooters have more than one gun and change as the seasons do. Others find that it's possible to fit their gun with changeable stocks or recoil pads,

The drop of a gunstock is a critical measurement, since it is the vertical measurement that aligns the eyes down the rib of the gun.

which would allow them to use the same gun for a variety of needs and differences in climate.

The simplest way to change the length of pull with the seasons, however, is with spacers that can be positioned between the butt plate and the recoil pad or by having interchangeable pads of different thickness. These can easily be changed with a screwdriver, and will allow the shooter to use his favorite scattergun year round. You will want to have the spacers sanded and the pad fitted to match the contour of the butt of the gun for both cosmetic and safety reasons.

If a shooter finds that his length is uncomfortable, he can move his forearm hand forward slightly to make the gun feel longer and back a bit to make it shorter. This should be considered temporary however, as proper positioning of the hand near the center of the forearm seems to work best for the majority of shooters. Additionally, bringing the hand too far back can result in unnecessary

A proper fit makes shooting in lightweight clothing much more comfortable.

Heavy clothing can be a factor in gun mounts if you don't adjust the forearm hand on the gun or shorten the length of pull to compensate for the added padding of the clothing.

muzzle dip, while moving it too far forward can inhibit the ease of the gun mount.

The best way to determine where to position the hand on the forearm of the gun is to place the gun in the shoulder for a vertical shot. The reason for this is that the most extension a shooter ever experiences is on a shot taken in the vertical position. With the gun mounted and placed vertically, drop the forearm hand to the waist. Then simply bring the forearm hand back up to the gun without stretching. The spot where the hand grabs the gun will be where it should be positioned for most shots.

DROP – THE VERTICAL ALIGNMENT

Without question, the most important measurement for gunfit is called drop. Drop is the vertical measurement of the gunstock that allows the master eye to look down the sighting plane of the barrel through the beads and beyond to the target, while the butt of the gun is mounted comfortably

Hand placement on the gun is critical to balancing the mount. Your greatest extension is vertical, so to determine where to put the forearm hand on the gun, start with a vertical setup.

With the gun vertical, simply reach up comfortably and grab the forearm. That will be the spot where you should hold the gun to insure consistent gun mounts.

Proper position of the forearm hand on a shotgun is important. When bringing the gun to the face in the mount, the forearm hand pushes the muzzle to the desired insertion point to start the lead picture sequence.

in the shoulder. Considering that the gun should always be brought to the face first with the mount, and as a result, to the shoulder, this measurement is typically taken in two or three spots along the top of the stock.

It must be remembered that a shotgun used for wingshooting has no rear sight. The master eye takes the place of that sight, and drop is the measurement that serves to align the two sights properly as the gun is mounted. And since a shotgun is pointed and not aimed, the correct drop will allow the eye and the gun to look to and shoot to the same spot.

Drop is measured at the comb, at the point of facial contact on the stock and at the heel or back of the stock. These three measurements assure that the gun is properly fitted vertically relative

the configuration of the shooter's body. When the drop of a stock is measured properly, the eye is aligned with the rib and the heel and toe of the stock comfortably conform to the shooter's shoulder makeup.

Shooters with long necks and sloping shoulders will generally need more drop at the heel of the gun than at the face. Short, stocky shooters typically require less drop at the heel. The difference is in the physical makeup of the individual.

The drop when measured where the face impacts the gun differs with high cheek bones and shallow cheek bones from person to person. These differences are small, but when it comes to getting the eye down the rib of the gun, an eighth of an inch can prove to be critical.

The drop in a stock is what aligns the eyes down the rib and the stock in the shoulder.

When looking down the barrel, most wingshooters want to see a tiny bit of the rib. This configuration will allow the shooter to keep the target in sight at all times just above the muzzle. When a shooter sees this sight picture, the gun should pattern in the range of 60/40, meaning that 60 percent of the pattern is above the center of the target and 40 percent off the pattern is below the target. If he sees less rib and right through the beads on the gun, the pattern will be more along the lines of 50/50. If he sees more of the rib, it would be closer to 70/30. Realistically, how the gun patterns for point of impact is a matter of personal preference for each shooter. If he is aware of a bit of rib, the consensus is that a small amount of lead is already built into the gun for the rising and driven shots typically encountered in many forms of wingshooting. And don't forget that seeing a bit of rib also allows the shooter to keep his target in view just above the muzzle at all times.

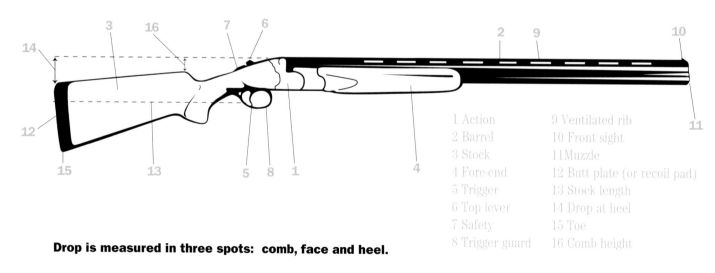

1 Action	9 Ventilated rib
2 Barrel	10 Front sight
3 Stock	11 Muzzle
4 Fore-end	12 Butt plate (or recoil pad)
5 Trigger	13 Stock length
6 Top lever	14 Drop at heel
7 Safety	15 Toe
8 Trigger guard	16 Comb height

Drop is measured in three spots: comb, face and heel.

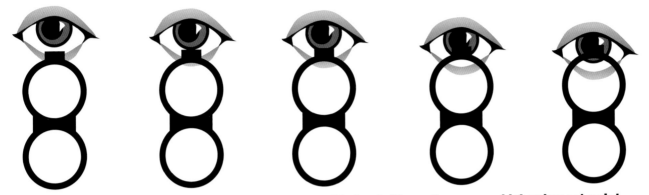

The more rib you see, the higher or lower the gun will shoot. More rib means a higher impact point, while less rib means a lower impact point. A look from the muzzle back to the shooter's eye will make the point. For hunting purposes, the fourth example of five is best. This is how the shooting eye should line up when the gun is properly fitted and mounted.

Because the drop at the facial contact point is so critical to the vertical alignment of the eye and the barrel, it would seem that this is the most important aspect of measuring drop for the shooter. It's easier for him to adapt to a gun that is too long or too short, or to one that doesn't perfectly align horizontally than it is to have a drop so low that he must lift his head to look down the barrel. The same can be said when the shooter has to bury his cheekbone into the comb to lower the eyes in order to compensate for a gun that shoots high.

When measuring drop a the heel, the butt of the gun should typically fit comfortably into the pocket of the shoulder, with the heel parallel to or just below the crown of the shoulder. This is generally pretty easy for shooters with square shoulders, but it can be a problem for shooters with either long necks or sloping shoulders. The tendency for

If the stock is too high on the shoulder, felt recoil will be increased.

By putting the gun fully in the shoulder pocket, the majority of the recoil will be absorbed in the body.

For those types of shooters with a standard off the rack gun is to either raise the shoulders as the gun is being mounted, or to mount the heel to high on the shoulder to compensate for their physical makeup. Both of those actions can cause severe recoil problems. When a portion of the heel of the stock shows above the shoulder, the entire surface area of the butt does not impact the shoulder, which could affect the recoil felt by the shooter and subsequently affect his ability to control the muzzle of the gun.

There are products on the market that can help adjust drop when needed. Perhaps the most common of these is the adjustable comb. This stock modification can raise or lower the comb so as to better position the eye down the rib of the gun.

There are also stick-on pads that can raise the drop on a gun should the shooter need to elevate the eye. If the stock is too high, a competent gunsmith or stocker should be able to take some of the wood off to lower it. Caution is advised here, however, because cutting a stock down should be done in small increments unless very precise measurements have been taken and shot using a try gun.

For complex fits, an adjustable comb might be an option. You can also change the impact points for trap, skeet, sporting or wingshooting with the twist of a wrench.

Aftermarket products like this comb raiser kit are perfect for fitting ladies and kids to stocks with a drop made for adult males.

Even though this factory stocked Beretta 20 gauge is a bit long for this shooter, the addition of the comb raiser puts the master eye correctly down the rib, making it much easier to shoot.

CAST – THE HORIZONTAL ALIGNMENT

One of the lesser known measurements for stock fitting is cast. This is the horizontal measurement that positions the gun to the left or right when mounted to align the eye down the rib of the gun. Since there is an offset distance between where the gun is mounted on the shoulder relative to the vertical position of the master eye on the face, it is sometimes necessary to modify the stock slightly. This is done by moving the stock either to the left or to the right in order to align the eye down the center of the rib. When a gun is cast to fit a particular shooter, this adjustment allows that shooter to mount the gun without having to cant his head slightly to move the eye in line with the rib. As a result, the shooter's head will remain almost perfectly still as the gun is mounted.

As you can see, the eye and shoulder pocket don't line up vertically. As a result, many guns offer a cast right or left in the stock.

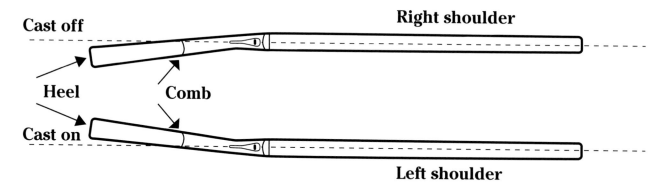

Cast off

Right shoulder

Heel

Comb

Cast on

Left shoulder

The cast in a stock is usually bent to the right for the right-hand shooter and to the left for the left-hand shooter. The bend in the stock compensates for the offset between the pocket of the shoulder and the base of the shooter's cheekbone when the gun is mounted.

In order to put cast into a gun, the stock is either bent to the right or left. A bend to the right moves the rib to the left when the gun is mounted to the face. This is called cast off and is generally suitable for most right hand shooters. A bend to the left is known as cast on and moves the rib to the right, which seems to suit left handed shooters more.

The majority of American-made guns come with little or no cast at all, which could explain why most of us are constantly reminded to keep our heads planted firmly in the gun. By firmly cheeking the stock, the master eye can be forced in line with the rib. Unfortunately when we press our cheek into the gun too hard, the result can be painful. Most experienced wingshooters can make a quick adjustment when using a gun that is not cast just right for them, but a properly fitted gun would eliminate the need for the adjustment. However, if the cast is too far off, it might cause the shooter's head to move around in order to position the eye down the center of the rib. When this happens, the chances of failure are magnified.

The fact is that many shooters fare well without cast, since many have learned to get the eye in line quickly as the gun is mounted. In many cases, the actually mount the gun slightly out of the shoulder pocket to compensate for a cast problem. This can cause an increase in the felt recoil of the gun, and leave a bruise on the outside of the shoulder if the mount is too far out, or on the collarbone if it is too far inside the pocket.

This is especially true for men with broad faces or shoulders, since the facial width or shoulder configuration tends to push the gun and sight plane farther away from the center of the eye than shooters with a slimmer build.

Most women also have cast problems, since they typically have to mount the gun farther out on the shoulder due to their physical makeup. In many instances, the cast of a lady's gun is greater at the toe of the stock than at the heel. You can see why a professional fitting for cast would most likely make the shooting experience more enjoyable.

PITCH – GETTING THE GUN IN THE SHOULDER

One of the important measurements that most shooters overlook is pitch. The pitch on a shotgun refers to the angle of the butt of the gun as it conforms to the shoulder of the shooter. It is really important for the entire surface of the butt of the gun to impact the shoulder when the gun is mounted. When the pitch is wrong on a gun, the shooter will likely feel more recoil. A fitter will look for the heel or bump and the toe of the stock to impact the shoulder simultaneously as the gun is mounted. If either the bump or the toe hit the shoulder visibly first, adjustments may be needed to insure the point of impact is what the shooter intended.

The pitch setup on a gun can be different for shooters who shoot flushing or crossing birds and those who shoot overhead driven birds. As the shoulder rotates vertically for the driven target, its surface changes, which will mean more or less

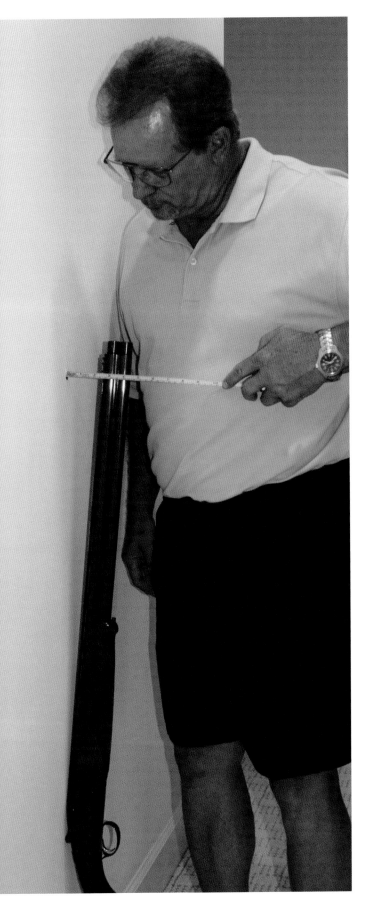

pitch depending on the makeup of the shooter.

Most game guns have down pitch, which means that if you stood the gun vertically against a wall in your home, and let the receiver touch the wall, the muzzle would face away from the wall. In most instances, the side by side would have more downward pitch than the over and under.

When the pitch is wrong the shooter will obviously feel that something is wrong. He will also see that there is a problem. When the pitch is too great, the muzzle will be lower than intended. If the pitch is too shallow, the muzzle will be higher than intended when the mount takes place.

GETTING YOUR GUN PROFESSIONALLY FITTED

There really aren't many quick fix gun fit remedies that the shooter can put in place without making some of the modifications alluded to earlier. Precise gun fit should be handled by a competent shooting professional or stock maker. This is best accomplished with the use of a try gun, which can be adjusted in many ways to insure the best fit possible.

One word of advice here about getting a gun properly fitted. Whether the modifications are being made directly to the gun in question or to a try gun if a stock is to be custom made, the gun should be shot while the fitting process is taking place. Most fitters use a pattern board with definitive target areas for this exercise, followed by a few shots at various clay pigeon presentations as the measurements get more precise. Shots are taken starting with a low gun position as used in the field, and measurements are changed as the gun fit is dialed in and the shot patterns become more centered.

Fitting the gun simply by mounting it on the shoulder and making adjustments from there can pose problems down the road. In most cases, shooters will not mount the gun the same way on a range with live fire as they will in a more cosmetic environment where no shot is taken. Keep in mind too that things like improper mounts, weight loss or gain and changes in the thickness of one's clothing will affect the fit of the gun.

Most impact patterning for gun fit is done at a distance of about 16 yards. Once the desired point of impact is reached at that distance, the shooter can move back in 10 yard increments, making sure that the gun consistently shoots where he looks. After a few shots at various clay presentations, if all is well, chances are the fit is dialed in almost perfectly. And once that is accomplished, you can bet the result will be an increase in one's success afield.

A word of caution must be interjected here. In order to properly impact pattern for perfect fit, the shooter's gun mount mechanics must be solid. If the gun isn't mounted in the same place on the face and shoulder time after time, the proper fit cannot be realized and the inconsistencies will persist.

WHAT ABOUT MOM AND THE KIDS?

If there was ever a can of worms opened by the shooting industry, it has to be the one where guns that were made for men were pushed on lady and youth shooters. Over the years some efforts have been made to build a gun that would actually fit an individual in these shooter groups. Just shortening the length of pull on a gun made for an adult male doesn't get the job done, as the physical makeup of shooters in these groups is usually quite different from that of the average male shooter.

A properly mounted gun should look the same in the hands of all shooters. Most of the time the gun fits for these groups is so bad that we're accustomed to seeing them roll their heads across the comb because it is too low or strain to lift the gun to their face because it is too heavy. There simply has to be a better way.

Physically these two groups are similar in that they usually need a higher comb and shorter stock for comfort. Both women and children tend to be blessed with high cheekbones and sloping shoulders, so the high comb allows the eye to look down the rib instead of under the rib and into the re-

The Beretta 391RL was designed for ladies and kids. The fit right out of the box is nearly perfect for this shooter.

Bad fits are obvious. The shooter will look noticeably uncomfortable holding and mounting the gun.

ceiver. Women usually find that they need more cast at the toe of the gun to get around the breast.

There are models currently available which will more closely fit the lady and youth shooters. Guns like the Beretta 391RL take some of these fit differences into consideration. The answer for these markets is not simply a smaller gauge gun for less recoil, less weight and a shorter stock. A proper fit would help insure that the first shooting experience for mom and the kids is a positive one, and the sooner we understand that, the sooner the next generation of shooters will be discovered.

Names of qualified fitters can be found by talking with the more knowledgeable gun shop owners in a given area, or by getting a recommendation at a local shooting facility or from one of the clay pigeon sanctioning bodies. Keep in mind, however, that proper gun fitting is much more than putting on a recoil pad, so get references and check them out before you proceed.

A properly fitted gun will instantly make the shooter better, as for the first time in his shooting career, the gun will actually shoot exactly where he looks.

A proper fit for a lady allows the shooter to focus through the gun without having to move the head around to line up the beads on the rib. Note the eye elevation in this photo. While not a perfect fit, it is far better than most lady shooters are faced with when shooting a shotgun made for the masses.

Ammo Selection and Performance

If there's any place where you can get more opinions than in the neighborhood beauty salon, it has to be around the ammo counter at your local sporting goods store. It is really fun to listen to shooters discuss which brand of ammo or load they plan to use for a given wingshooting excursion. It is not uncommon to hear a little bit of everything in this scenario, since many shooters tend to make ammo choices based on what their ancestors told them was best. However, an ammo choice that was really good a generation ago may not be the best choice today.

Certainly one of the more important aspects of wingshooting is making the right choice of ammunition to get the job done when shooting a specific game bird. Unfortunately many shooters tend to be more concerned with the price of ammunition rather than its efficiency. That's not to say that the less expensive promo loads won't get the job done. In many instances they are perfectly acceptable, especially when hunting the smaller bird species. You will find that if you get the muzzle of the gun in the right place when the shot is taken, virtually any ammo will do the job.

While shooters are often force fed a steady diet of price sensitive loads, shooters who opt for the more premium loads have been led to believe that bigger is always better when it comes to shooting live birds. As a result they often simply grab anything off the shelf with MAGNUM or HIGH BRASS written on it, feeling that they gain a distinct advantage. There are many myths in the outdoor community concerning ammunition and its performance, and this chapter will dispel some of them.

UNDERSTANDING SHOT SHELL CHARACTERISTICS

First of all, it is prudent to say that shot shell performance for the standard hunting load for all gauges, 10 to .410 is essentially the same in terms of pellet velocity and down range penetration performance. The basic difference between gauges is in the size of the bore diameter and the measured amount of powder, shot and other components that make up various loads. These differences mean that when considering the variety of hunting loads available, there can be variances of more than 300 feet per second between the lowest and highest advertised velocities of shot shells for hunting across the board. Think about that. We're talking about a difference in the length of a football field per second between the pellet speed of the fastest hunting loads versus the slowest available loads. These speeds are usually measured as the shot emerges from the muzzle or out to a distance of about three feet ahead of the muzzle.

Here's the scary part of this statement. The human eye simply cannot discern the difference in lead on a target up to around 35 yards away when using the slowest and fastest hunting loads. The faster loads tend to slow down more quickly because their speed builds up more resistance in air than would a slower load.

I can distinctly remember shooting a 25 straight skeet round with a Winchester Featherlite load that posted a velocity of 980 feet per second. As an experienced competitive skeet shooter for a number of years, my skeet leads were pretty much memorized. I had never shot a load that slow,

One of the more important aspects of wingshooting is making the right choice of ammunition.

but I did not change my lead on any target while shooting that perfect round. The lead pictures were the same as if I was shooting my normal 1,200 feet per second target loads.

The major difference in the posted velocities of different loads is how well they cleanly harvest game. Birds are cleanly harvested when there is sufficient pellet energy placed on the target. The further and larger the bird being shot is, the more important speed, pellet size and pattern density bcomes. As a result, the slower velocity loads might not be as functional as those loads with higher velocities.

To put the differences between the gauges into proper perspective, the larger the gauge, the more payload it is capable of delivering to a speeding bird or clay target. And the more pellets the shooter can deliver to his target, the better are his chances of making a clean kill. Rest assured, however, that bigger the better theory is not necessarily the end of all means when it comes to success in the field. It is not the size of the load that makes the difference. The determining factor is the number of pellets that the choke and load combination can deliver into the vital areas of a bird, coupled with the amount of penetration and dispensed energy the pellets place on the bird being shot. It will be these variables, plus the velocity of those pellets, that ultimately decides whether a bird is cleanly harvested or not when the proper lead picture is executed by the shooter.

If you consider that the pellet velocity for a 12 gauge load and a .410 gauge load could travel at the same speed, the larger number of pellets in the 12 gauge load would obviously give the shooter an edge on live birds. Without question, a centered hit from the 12 gauge will give the shooter more killing power than the .410 on sheer pellet volume alone. If the shooter can better understand how his ammunition performs under certain conditions and why, he will make wiser choices concerning which loads work best for each of the various gamebirds he intends to hunt.

It's a pretty safe bet that all wingshooters want to make clean kills when they take a shot. This is certainly more possible when the pellet(s) strike the target in a lethal area. Many shooters will find very few signs of pellet strikes when they clean their harvested game, so the location of those hits and how they penetrate the bird are of critical importance.

Let's then take a look at some of the facts about shot shell performance that ultimately affect the success of a shot. First of all, a shooter should understand that the recoil and muzzle jump he feels when the trigger is pulled is a direct result of the primer igniting the powder charge in the shot shell. On the other end of the gun, the shot charge is exiting the muzzle and flying towards its target at more than 800 miles per hour.

Most shooters would think that the more powder a shell contains, the more recoil it can

There's a noticeable difference in the size of the ammo from different gauges, but not always a huge difference in the payload and performance.

generate. To a certain extent, this is true, but felt recoil is dependent as much on the pressure or burn curve it generates when ignited as it is on the powder volume. A fast burning powder usually has a higher pressure curve than a slow burning powder. A sharp pressure curve usually denotes a quicker burn and sharper felt recoil. An elongated pressure curve found in the more progressive burning powders would indicate that the recoil be more spread out over time and a bit less felt recoil therefore results.

Another important consideration when choosing a shot shell is the heavier the shot charge you choose, the more the recoil you're likely to feel. With a proper gun fit and mount, shooters can lessen the felt recoil of heavier loads, but when you add weight, you increase recoil. Sir Isaac Newton had it right when he stated that for every

action, there is an opposite and equal reaction. Recoil and muzzle jump are both a direct result of mass versus energy, so shooters should be aware that by increasing the weight of the shot charge they stand to increase the felt recoil of the gun.

It is what happens inside of the bore, however, that determines the down range performance of the shooter's chosen load. When the trigger is pulled and the shot shell primer ignites the powder, a tremendous amount of energy is squeezed into a small space. Most of the shot shells used worldwide contain lead pellets. Lead is a very soft metal, and the round pellets in a shot shell are easily deformed as a result of this internal pressure. This pellet deformation is primarily what causes the pellets to form a pattern and string out as they fly towards the target. The resistance of air and wind also play a part, but pellet deformation is usually the primary factor in how a load patterns out of a given choke.

The pellets in steel and tungsten based loads used primarily for waterfowl and some upland birds are much harder than lead. Steel pellets are lighter than their lead counterparts, so a larger pellet is recommended to give the shooter the same impact a smaller lead pellet. The tungsten-based loads tend to be heavier than lead, so the same size or one size smaller pellet than with lead is recommended. The harder pellets tend to pattern tighter with shorter shot strings than those found with lead loads because they don't lose their shape

Over the years, hundreds of tests have been conducted to help optimize shot shell performance for both clay targets and gamebirds. These tests have consistently proven that there is a direct correlation between the hardness of the shot charge pellets, their retained velocity and the consistency of pattern that the gun delivers.

As internal pressures increase, so do those chances for pellet deformation in lead ammunition. So while heavier loads and greater pellet velocity might mean improved performance, they also mean that less pellets could reach the target since so many are deformed as the powder ignites and fall away from the core of the pattern. Let's

face it. Round pellets fly straighter than those with flat spots caused by the tremendous energy transfer in the chamber of the gun when the trigger is pulled.

Fortunately, shot shell manufacturers have discovered ways to improve the performance of their loads. The powders used today insure that the shot charge can reach its maximum velocity while in the confines of the barrel. In fact, the powder charge usually achieves a complete burn in the first 18 inches of the barrel, while pressures continue to increase behind the shot charge as the load moves through the barrel. Plastic shot cups have significantly improved pattern efficiencies by virtually eliminating the metal to metal contact that was the norm for the predecessors of the modern shot shell load. By taking away this abrasive action, pellets are no longer deformed significantly by the internal walls of the barrel as they might have been decades ago.

Since lead is such a soft metal, the addition of antimony, a hardening agent for lead, greatly reduces the pellet deformation found in chilled or non-hardened shot. Other improvements include copper or nickel plated shot, which adds a hard coating to the pellets, and buffered loads which serve as a cushion to reduce the pellet deformation as the powder ignition takes place. Both antimony and plating increase the hardness of the pellets so they fly straighter and pattern better.

The performance between inexpensive promotional loads and a quality field load can be markedly different. Many hunters opt to go with the cheaper loads because of price, but there is no doubt that they are giving up something in performance, especially at longer ranges.

Just as there are differences between a high performance model of a certain car brand and the generic basic model of that same brand, there are differences in the makeup of shot shells too. The major difference usually comes from the type of wad column used and the amount of antimony mixed in when the pellets are formed.

Promotional loads typically have less than two percent antimony content and a short, thin walled shot cup, if they have one at all. On the other hand, premium loads come with five to eight percent antimony and a longer, stiffer shot cup. Reloaders often choose magnum shot over chilled shot because the magnum pellet is harder. Just as both models of the aforementioned car will get the driver from point to point, so too will both shot shells go bang and deliver the pellets to their target. The difference between the two lies in the performance efficiency by which the job gets done, and buyers should expect to pay a more premium price for better performance.

WEATHER AND ITS EFFECTS ON SHOT SHELL PERFORMANCE

Shot shell performance can be significantly affected by changes in weather conditions such as extreme hot or cold, high humidity and wind. These factors are beyond the shooter's control and, as a result, he should be aware of these potential performance changes.

Perhaps the worst conditions for shot shell performance would be cold air with high humidity. Extremely cold air does affect the burning characteristics of powder, and high humidity can affect shot velocity and how a load patterns. Consider that in outer space, where there is no air density or humidity, scientists have theorized that there would be no contributing factors for pattern or shot string formation. As a result, the shot would emerge from the barrel still in the confines of the shot cup and potentially could stay that way to infinity.

The best shooting conditions occur in the high, thinner air found at altitude with low humidity and average temperatures. Under these conditions, ammunition performs at a level that exceeds its performance at sea level. Shooters can expect to experience a definite improvement in their shot shell performance characteristics under these conditions, as velocities stay up longer and patterns tend to hold tighter.

Strong winds also have an affect on how a load performs. A tail wind will help hold a pattern together longer, which will improve the pattern's performance. On the other hand, a head wind will slow down pellet velocities more quickly and typi-

cally cause the pattern to open up more. A crosswind can move a shot string left or right, with the smaller shot sizes being more easily affected.

I distinctly remember an incident that opened my eyes on the shot drift in high winds. While duck hunting in Argentina a few years ago, I downed a bird that needed to be finished off quickly. We were hunting in a large open water area and there was a strong 30 miles per hour crosswind blowing when I took the shot. My load of one ounce number fives splashed about three feet to the left of the bird. I was shooting an improved modified choke, and the bird was only about 35 yards away.

Climatic and geographic differences will affect the performance of shotshell loads. Extreme altitude and cold temperatures seem to have the most affect.

Needless to say, my hunting partner and I were surprised at the pellet drift at that distance.

Of course, the target distance is a determining factor of how much a shot string moves. Keep in mind that 7½ shot is 66 percent heavier than number nine shot, so it's easy to see why weather conditions can affect the performance characteristics of a particular load. When you consider how much the number five pellets moved in the aforementioned example, it stands to reason that smaller pellets can be moved around even more by windy conditions.

CHOOSING THE RIGHT LOAD

As you can see, many factors play a role in making today's shotgun ammunition better than ever, but with so many shot shell options available, how does one go about choosing the right load for his

gun and for the game bird he plans to hunt? Let's take a look at some of the variables that affect those decisions.

When a wingshooter has to make decisions regarding the type of load and shot size he needs for his hunting needs, the choices are seemingly endless. His shot shell decisions, however, should be made based on the size of the birds he will be hunting and the distances that he expects most of his shots to be taken. The larger the bird, the larger the shot size in most cases. On longer shots you might want to consider a larger shot size with a higher velocity. The reasons for this are obvious. Larger birds are more easily harvested with larger shot and, at distance, the larger shot sizes retain their down range velocity longer and tend to pattern better. Loads with smaller pellets will also harvest larger birds, but as distances increase the smaller pellets bleed off energy quickly, which leads to reduced performance.

It has been previously established that regardless of the gauge, choke, target size or its distance, the down range performance of a shotgun load is largely determined by the roundness of the pellets. This is especially true for shots beyond 35 yards, since deformed pellets slow down more quickly and do not fly as true as round pellets. As a result, quality ammunition with hard shot will always be preferred for long distance shooting and tighter patterns for big gamebirds.

Some hunters, however, prefer to use loads filled with chilled or soft lead shot. This is the case with many upland bird hunters. The average shot they take will typically in the 20-30 yard range. The pellet deformation that occurs in the chilled shot loads actually means that the pattern will open up more quickly, giving better coverage of the bird at close range.

Most wingshooters will change loads as the season for their intended quarry progresses. For instance, early season mourning dove shooting generally means a larger number of young birds at fairly close range, so lighter loads and smaller shot will typically get the job done. As the birds get older, smarter and larger, those hunted later in the season might be more easily taken with heavier loads and larger shot.

Shot size recommendations

Upland Game	Shot size recommendation
Pheasant	4, 5, 6
Chukar, Grouse, Partridge	6, 7-1/2
Quail	7-1/2, 8
Dove	7-1/2, 8
Rail, Snipe, Woodcock	7-1/2, 8
Pigeon	5, 6, 7-1/2

Waterfowl (steel shot)	Shot size recommendation
Geese	BBB, BB, 1
Ducks (over decoys)	2, 3, 4
Ducks (pass shooting)	BB, 1, 2

Waterfowl (tungsten alloy shot, Hevi-shot)	Shot size recommendation
Geese	BB, 2
Ducks (over decoys)	4, 5, 6
Ducks (pass shooting)	2, 4, 5

Pheasant hunters often start the season with number six or even seven and a half shot, but when the snows come and the birds get smarter, older and more wary, they generally go to number four or five shot. The larger shot retains velocity and energy longer, and can be helpful on wild flushing roosters.

IS BIGGER REALLY BETTER?

Many hunters have grown up thinking that bigger has to be better. In some instances that is certainly the case, especially when it comes to shooting large gamebirds. The problem with larger loads, however, is that they typically come with greater recoil and often lower velocities. Let's analyze what this really means when it comes to shotgunning.

To many hunters, bigger simply means going from a 20 gauge to a 12 gauge, or from a 12 gauge to a three and a half inch 12 or 10 gauge. The old adage follows that the bigger the gauge, the more killing power it has. On the positive side, the bigger gauges often heavier loads, which mean more pellets in the pattern.

A second consideration of "bigger" usually means choosing a heavier shot charge, but there's no free lunch on that one. Shotguns are not outside the laws of physics, so the shooter should realize that by using a heavier load, he will also have to increase the powder charge in order to maintain the velocity of the load he is replacing. Don't forget that in most instances when you add shot weight or powder to a load, you also increase recoil. The only way to reduce recoil from a load is to lighten the shot weight, reduce the powder charge or change the powder to one with lower pressure readings.

Most hunters are limited to choosing from the loads they find in their local sporting goods stores. As a result, they are leaving their ammo choice to someone else. Some hunters choose to reload their own ammo. There are many different load recipes available to the reloader. If you choose this route for your ammo, make sure you follow the loading instructions provided by your chosen powder manufacturer.

So how does a hunter find a comfort zone with his chosen load? Well, in today's marketplace, wingshooters will find that some manufacturers want to promote high velocity, deep penetrating loads, while others push loads with lower velocities and superior patterning characteristics. Both types of loads have their pluses and minuses, and which type the shooter chooses is solely dependent on what conditions he will face while hunting.

Tests have shown that the lower velocity loads offer better patterns since the chamber pressures generated when fired are usually lower than their high velocity counterparts. The results of such a load are less pellet deformation on ignition and subsequently better downrange pattern performance. Unfortunately the slower velocities generated by such loads also mean that they will lack the down range penetration power needed to cleanly harvest

Pellet counts for one ounce of lead shot

Type	Pelletcount
2	87
4	135
5	170
6	225
7-1/2	350
8	410
8-1/2	497
9	58

Pellet counts for one ounce of steel shot

Type	Pelletcount
BBB	62
BB	72
1	103
2	125
3	158
4	192
6	315

Many hunters and recreational shooters enjoy reloading. There are scores of load combinations available from powder manufacturers. Just make sure you follow their recipe precisely.

many gamebirds as shot distances increase. As a result, these lower velocity shells (1,175 feet per second and lower) are recommended for shots taken 30 yards and under. They are perfect for smaller upland birds such as quail, woodcock, grouse in heavy timber and early season doves.

In heavily wooded shooting conditions, hunters might find that one or two shot sizes larger than they would normally use in open terrain might be beneficial. Larger shot will push through leaves and branches in thick cover, and certainly has more knockdown and penetrating power. Using these loads under these conditions will result in less cripples and more birds in the bag in the long run. Some will agree that you need to push the shot through cover, so they go with the larger shot size. Others will contend that putting more pellets in the pattern will get the job done, so they choose a slightly smaller shot size.

On extremely close shots, some manufacturers have developed spreader loads that offer wide pattern coverage at ranges under 20 yards, even with a full choke. These loads are particularly effective for the first shot on smaller gamebirds like quail and woodcock, since skeet type patterns are possible at these very close ranges.

The higher velocity loads will prove to be better on larger gamebirds such as pheasant, chukar, partridge and larger species of grouse. For the most part these types of birds tend to be hunted in more open terrain and longer shots are not the exception, they are the rule.

Perhaps the biggest advantage to higher velocity loads is the increase in down range penetration, which leads to cleaner kills at distance. The shooter should keep in mind, though, that higher velocity usually means more chance of pellet deformation in the shot charge, unless he is using a harder shot such as copper or nickel plated lead, so a bit more choke might be necessary when shooting high velocity ammunition. Just to be sure, a bit of pattern testing will most likely clear up any performance questions the shooter might have.

Since wingshooters often make the mistake of purchasing ammunition based on cost rather than quality, let's take a look at what you get for your investment. Don't forget that both the inexpensive promotional loads the manufacturers flood the market with annually and the higher priced tighter patterning loads can be a hindrance to a shooter when used in the wrong situation. Their patterning characteristics should be checked before venturing afield for a hunt at the distances you plan to take most of your shots.

Don't think that this a suggestion that these loads won't kill birds. You can bet they will. It's just best to know that if you do your job, the load you've selected will do its job. Keep in mind that shooters will find that quality ammunition with hardened, coated or buffered shot will give them significant performance improvements in virtually all cases. And with no more shots than most wingshooters get in a season, the small difference in cost is more than offset by better performance.

WATERFOWL LOADS - UNDERSTANDING NON-TOXIC SHOT PERFORMANCE

Without question, waterfowlers were treated to a shock in the late 1980s and early 1990s when non-toxic shot became mandatory for waterfowl hunting throughout America. It's a good bet that non-toxic loads will become the standard for

There are many options when it comes to waterfowl loads. Making the right choice for your type of shooting is very important.

upland birds in many areas in the near future as well. As a result, there's no need here to argue the positives and negatives of steel, bismuth, Hevi-Shot or other non-toxic shot products versus lead, since it's a given that those types of loads are here to stay. We should simply accept their existence and take the time to understand their performance characteristics and learn to shoot them.

The major difference between lead and the other non-toxic loads presently available is the weight of the shot. Steel pellets are only 71 percent as dense as their lead counterparts. This difference has proven to have an affect on pellet velocities and their down range penetration power on large birds such as ducks and geese. When using steel shot loads, hunters were forced to use larger shot sizes than they might have typically chosen in order to compensate for the differences in shot weight between steel and lead.

Of course, steel is much harder than lead, so shooters experienced no pellet deformation to effect patterns as had been the case with lead loads. In fact, the steel loads tended to pattern much tighter using more open chokes than those used to enhance lead loads.

The first steel loads offered pretty high velocities, but they lacked the acceptable performance characteristics that most hunters demanded. In many instances, the lack of acceptance was primarily due to an overall lack of knowledge about the new loads. Many shooters tried to shoot them just as they would their favorite lead loads, which proved to be a recipe for disaster. Keep in mind, the manufacturers were learning how to make these loads, just as shooters were learning how to shoot them. The shells were fine at close range, but seemed to blow patterns at the distances where waterfowlers had been comfortable with lead loads. In addition, the hardness of the larger steel pellets being forced down a shotgun barrel at such speeds damaged some shotgun barrels. Needless to say, many hunters were frustrated, and some either refused to shoot it and/or gave up waterfowl hunting all together.

Fortunately, steel loads have been significantly improved over the years, and hunters now have a better understanding of how to shoot them. Most hunters now know that the steel pellets they were using were lighter than lead, and to get the same down range ballistics and penetration power of their lead loads they could choose a steel load that was about two sizes larger than what they used with lead.

While this is still the accepted norm for steel shot selection, some knowledgeable gunners have elected to shoot steel loads that are three or four sizes larger than what they would have used with lead. This is especially the case for big ducks like mallards, blacks or large sea ducks in more open water shooting conditions. The down range penetration power of number one or BB shot has proven to reduce the number of cripples on such large duck species. Of course a load with less pellets put a greater demand on the shooter's ability to deliver the pattern on the bird.

The biggest complaint registered by hunters was that steel loads wounded more birds than might have when using lead loads. There are a couple of reasons that such concerns might be true. First of all, the steel pellets in a shot shell are round and very hard. As a result, there is virtually no pellet deformation, which minimizes innternal hemorrhaging for a quick harvest.

The hard pellets also mean that the shot string of a steel load is much shorter than that in a lead load. It also means that a more open choke than you might have used with your lead loads will

Waterfowl hunting is available in many countries. These yellow bill ducks were taken in South Africa.

Shotshell Pellet Energy Comparisons

Listed below are pellet energy comparisons for lead, Hevi-Shot and steel waterfowl loads. Tungsten based loads like Winchester Extended Range will have similar energy ratings to Hevi-Shot.

Experts suggest that it takes multiple pellets delivering 2.35-2.40 foot pounds of energy per square inch to cleanly harvest a mallard duck. Here are pellet energy ratings at 40 and 60 yards.

Type Shot	Shot Size	Muzzle Velocity	Retained Energy (ftlb/sqinch)	
			40 yards	60 Yards
Lead	7 ½	1,330 fps	1.4	0.9
	6	1,330 fps	2.5	1.7
	5	1,330 fps	3.6	2.5
	4	1,330 fps	4.8	3.4
	2	1,330 fps	8.0	5.8
Hevi-Shot	7	1,325 fps	1.6	0.9
	6	1,325 fpsa	2.8	1.7
	5	1,325 fps	3.9	2.5
	4	1,325 fps	5.3	3.5
	2	1,325 fps	9.1	6.2
Steel	6	1,365 fps	1.3	0.2
	4	1,365 fps	2.4	1.4
	2	1,275 fps	4.1	2.4
	2	1,365 fps	4.4	2.6
	BB	1,275 fps	8.3	5.2
	T	1,300 fps	12.5	8.0

deliver excellent patterns with steel. These differences take some getting used to.

Tighter patterns and shorter shot strings mean less room for shooter error. And many shooters just struggled with how far a steel load would cleanly harvest a bird. These variables had a great deal to do with wounded birds. Fortunately the education process for shooting steel has helped shooters improve their success in the duck blind.

As ammo companies tested and further developed steel loads, they determined that by increasing the speed of the pellets, they could increase the distances that steel could cleanly harvest a bird. High speed steel loads are now more the norm than the exception, and hunters have discovered that the extra penetrating power of high speed loads can

make a considerable difference in the downrange killing performance of a given load.

Shooters should definitely test a variety of steel loads using different chokes in order to get a good reading on what their waterfowl gun shoots best. There can be significant performance differences between chokes, loads and various brands of ammunition. This is especially true when using high speed steel, since these loads may require slightly different choke restrictions to match the patterning performance of standard velocity steel.

In recent years, bismuth and tungsten based shot have been approved as a non-toxic substitutes for lead. Bismuth is a gray metallic element that is removed during the smelting process of ores containing metals such as gold, silver, lead, copper, etc. Since it is more than 90 percent as dense as lead, it offers a similar consistency to lead. Bismuth tends to be brittle, so the shot is alloyed with three percent tin for hardness. Waterfowlers who prefer the smaller gauges or shooting their older vintage guns tend to like it because it because it is soft enough to use in most modern shotguns. Bismuth is available in gauges from 10 to .410, which gives shooters a wide selection of loads for waterfowl that are not available in other non-toxic options.

Tungsten-Iron was developed into a viable waterfowl load after steel and bismuth, but since it is 94 percent as dense as lead, many shooters warmed up to it quickly. A unique characteristic of tungsten, however, is its hardness. Believe it or not, it is more than twice as hard as steel, and over 20 times as hard as lead. This remarkable hardness causes tungsten-iron loads to require a very thick shot cup since any metal to metal contact within the bore of a shotgun could cause barrel damage. These thick shot cups reduce the amount of pellets that can be placed in a load, but fewer pellets mean greater velocity and their hardness result in very tight patterns at some pretty remarkable distances.

Another tungsten shot that is being used is tungsten polymer, which is found in such loads as Kent Tungsten Matrix. This shot is ballistically similar to lead since its density is essentially the same. It is also only slightly harder than lead, so hunters have to look closely to find any discernible differences between tungsten polymer and their old lead loads.

The new kid on the block is called Hevi-Shot. It too is a blend of metals, including tungsten, and is actually heavier than lead. Strangely enough, the pellets in a Hevi-Shot load are not round, but they tend to produce very tight patterns. Hevi-Shot is about the same hardness as tungsten iron, so a more open choke will usually produce excellent patterns for harvesting waterfowl.

And since the shot is heavier than lead, the pellets tend to retain their down range killing power at distances greater than lead. Because of this phenomenon shooters report taking waterfowl at extreme distances.

Not to be outdone, other manufacturers looked to develop their own alternative to steel. With names like High Density and Extended Range, these new pellets are up to 25 percent heavier than steel; even heavier than lead. They are also softer than steel, which means that they can be shot in any barrel approved for steel shot. Over time, the big three ammo makers in the U.S. (Winchester, Remington and Federal) all developed shot that is heavier than lead and offers tremendous patterning characteristics.

The bad news is that these alternatives to steel tend to be expensive to mine and develop into the shot used for waterfowl shooting. As a result, they are generally far more expensive for the consumer, as was steel when it was first introduced. As time passes and the loads are available in higher quantity, there's a chance that the price could moderate slightly. One thing is for certain, however, with the cost of non-toxic shot where it is, waterfowlers are having to become more proficient with the gun.

Since these lead alternatives are closer to lead in weight and performance than steel, hunters might consider using the same shot size they would with lead. And because they are heavier that steel, hunters will likely feel more recoil than they did from the lighter weight steel loads.

Another drawback to steel loads was that the hardness of the pellets tended to pass through birds. Since there were no edges formed on the shot by pellet deformation and no pellet expansion as was the case with lead, there was little chance of internal hemorrhaging and a quick harvest. Pellets like bismuth and tungsten polymer performed more like lead, and the heavier tungsten iron and heavier than lead pellets tended to have more of a shocking effect on birds. As discussed, shooters who stuck with steel, moved to the larger pellets to get the same bird harvesting effect.

When it comes to making choices for chokes and loads, non-toxic shot shells are no different than lead loads. They should all be patterned with a hunter's individual gun and choke combination in order to achieve the best performance characteristics possible. Once wingshooters gain confidence in how to shoot non-toxic loads, there's a good chance that the years of lead shot usage will be all but forgotten.

Barrels, Chokes and Patterning for Optimum Performance

hoosing the right ammunition is certainly a major step to making a successful shot in the field, and understanding how to fine tune the right load to the barrel and choke of a particular scattergun is sure to produce cleaner kills. It is very important for shooters to know that just because their forefathers or friends shot a particular load with success, doesn't necessarily mean that they can use that same combination with equal results. Shotgun barrels and chokes, even from identical model shotguns, do not generally perform equally, so in order to maximize the capabilities of a scattergun the shooter has to perform some tests in order to get the most from his gun.

This book is not about the intricacies of how shot shell components work to allow a successful shot. Having the basic knowledge of how the shot travels from the shell to its intended target, however, will give shooters a better grasp of the importance of fine tuning their guns to specific chokes and loads.

WHAT HAPPENS WHEN THE GUN GOES BANG?

When a shotgun shell is fired, a number of interesting things happen within the bore. First of all, there is a violent action and reaction that stems from the ignition of a powder charge that sends a shot column of pellets speeding out of the barrel.

Shot shells that are placed in the barrel chamber are larger than the bore diameter of that barrel. As a result most factory barrels are made with a tapered section one half inch or so in front of the shot shell that squeezes the payload into the smaller muzzle diameter. This taper is called a forcing cone.

The forcing cone in shotguns was initially necessary because the early loads used felt or paper wads to separate the powder charge from the shot. Since the chamber of a shotgun is slightly larger than the bore diameter, gases from the powder ignition could escape around the early wad designs, which resulted in a loss of performance.

Modern shotgun barrels are designed to allow a shell component transition from the chamber to the bore of the barrel, through the choke and to the target. Note the gradual taper of the forcing cone just past the chamber of the barrel. Many hunters have the forcing cone lengthened to lessen felt recoil and improve patterns. Some shotgun manufacturers offer an elongated forcing cone in some of their models.

Today's advanced shot cups are designed to seal those gases behind the shot column, so the forcing cone is not as critical as it was some years ago. Even so, most shotguns still come with a noticeable forcing cone in place. You can actually see the cone if you hold the barrel up to a light source and look through the barrel from the receiver end. You'll notice what looks like a ring at the end of the chamber. That would be the reflective image of the forcing cone.

The standard bore diameter of a 12 gauge shotgun barrel is .729 or slightly less than three quarters of an inch in diameter. Some manufacturers' barrels are actually smaller in diameter, while others come with an overbore that measures .735 to .745. The term overbore simply means that the bore is larger than the accepted standard of that manufacturer's 12 gauge barrel. Many of today's clay target guns and select hunting guns come with these overbored barrels, which the experts claim lessen pellet deformation, improve patterns and decrease felt recoil.

A shotgun can be effectively bored only to a diameter that allows the wad column behind the shot charge to properly seal in the gases formed by burning gunpowder, which is how the pellets get their velocity and subsequent downrange performance. The firing of a shotgun shell can generate forces within the bore upwards of 10,000 pounds of pressure per square inch. When this intense pressure hits the back of the wad column like a sledgehammer, the violent reaction causes the lower pellets in the wad to slam into the stationary upper pellets. Depending on the type of shot being used, the flat spotting or pellet deformation discussed earlier can occur. And once the shot charge encounters the force cone, additional deformation is usually the result since it is being squeezed into a smaller area. All of this internal action is the foundation of the shot string and pattern that the gun shoots.

THE LONG AND SHORT OF SHOT STRINGS

When the shot column exits the shell hull, it encounters the forcing cone and additional pellet deformation occurs depending on the length and angle of the cone. The burning powder exerts heavy outward pressure as the pellets are pushed forward. Slower burning powders usually cause less deformation than the faster burning varieties.

Contrary to what many hunters believe, the shot charge remains in the wad column for the entire length of the barrel and only starts to form a shot string and pattern after it exits the muzzle and encounters air resistance. You would think that the more restriction a barrel bore and choke has, the longer the shot string will be when it is formed. Not so. There's more to it than that. You will find that the .410 bore has the longest shot string of any gauge, which is why it is the least forgiving of all gauges to shoot.

Regardless of what choke the shooter has in his gun, a shot string will always be formed once the pellets encounter the atmosphere. Keep in mind that the rounder the pellets are when they encounter air, the tighter the pattern will be at distance. Deformed pellets will bleed off energy and speed more quickly than round ones, and they have a tendency to fly away from the center core of the pattern. This is what forms the shotstring, which can be as long as six to eight feet or more from front to back 40 yards from the muzzle.

But does the shotstring help or hurt the wingshooter? As you might imagine, there are differing trains of thought on this. When shooting birds, it would seem appropriate to get as many pellets to the target at the point of impact as possible to insure a clean kill.

This is probably more important on crossing shots than any other presentation a bird in flight can pose to the shooter, since the 90 degree angle is the toughest to center with a pattern. It is possible for a speeding bird crossing in front of a hunter to be impacted by only a portion of the shot string on long crossing birds if the lead picture isn't perfect. Remember that the pellets are traveling at a high rate of speed and the shot string will pass through the intended target very quickly. Even so, it is possible to miss a bird with the front of the string and hit it with the back of the string. This happens because a bird that presents itself at an angle to the shooter is constantly in motion, and if the shot was slightly in front of the target, that angle will close into the path of the pellets. If you're just in front of the bird you've got a chance

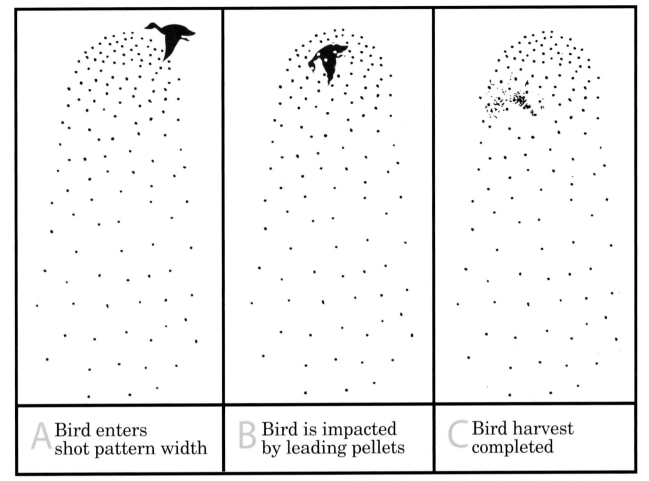

| A Bird enters shot pattern width | B Bird is impacted by leading pellets | C Bird harvest completed |

You've got a slight chance to hit a bird with the back of the shotstring if you misread the lead by a small distance. Steel shot shells tend to have a shorter shot string than lead because of the hardness of the pellets.

to hit it. If you're behind, you have no chance to hit it.

Because a shorter shot string will cause more pellets to hit a bird if the shooter's lead is correct, he has to be more precise when obtaining that proper forward allowance. On birds that typically fly away from the hunter (quail, partridge, grouse, pheasant, etc.), shot string length is not as important, since on birds moving away from the shooter, most of the shot charge will impact the bird with the proper sight picture.

MODIFICATIONS TO IMPROVE SHOT STRING EFFICIENCY

There are some relatively simple ways to greatly improve the efficiency of the shotstring produced by a shotgun. Perhaps the easiest way to improve this efficiency is to use higher quality ammunition. Buffered loads or lead loads with high antimony content will automatically improve how the gun patterns. Steel and tungsten iron shot and, to a lesser extent, bismuth, already have shorter shot strings than lead, since given the extreme hardness of those types of pellets there is little pellet deformation in the barrel.

Experienced gunsmiths and a scattering of aftermarket barrel modification companies can either lengthen the forcing cone or overbore the barrel of most guns. Without question the best of these modifications is the forcing cone extension. This simple procedure will contribute to the performance of just about any shotgun, because it will ease the transition of the shot from the chamber to the bore. Because of the back pressure

Porting has become popular with many clay shooters, and some factory models are delivered with ported barrels. There are a number of different aftermarket companies that port guns for hunters and clay shooters. The porting concept is designed to reduce the amount of muzzle jump when a shell is fired. The reduced muzzle jump allows shooters to recover for a second shot more quickly.

reduction realized during this transition, there will be less felt recoil and lower pellet deformation, which should result in better patterns and shorter shotstrings.

If you intend to have the forcing cone lengthened in your shotgun, check with the company doing the work to confirm that such modifications are possible on the gun. Some semiautomatic shotguns will be sensitive to any change in the pressures that have been compensated to operate the action of the gun.

One of the newer barrel modifications available today is backboring. This is the enlarging of the bore diameter of a shotgun, which primarily effects shotgun ballistics in a couple of ways. Keep in mind that overboring is done when the barrel is manufactured. It is manufactured with a bore that is over the accepted standard for that manufacturer. Backboring is an after market modification which actually cuts metal out of a smaller bore.

So how does backboring work? First of all, enlarging the bore gives the shot shell proponents more room to work, so powder gases can expand more, thereby converting chemical energy to kinetic energy. Second, by moving the proponents through an enlarged area, there is less friction between the wad and the bore wall of the barrel. As a result, pellet velocity can be increased and patterns improved, since the friction created as the pellets travel down the barrel is reduced. It is possible to buy as number of target guns and some hunting guns across the counter with this modification already done in the by overboring. Many shotguns currently in the hands of wingshooters

worldwide can be backbored by any number of companies specializing in barrel modifications. The caveat here is to make sure that the barrel wall thickness is sufficient to perform this modification.

It is important to note that the choke systems of shotgun barrels are fitted based on the original bore diameter of the barrel in question, so any bore changes will also constitute choke changes.

Of course any changes you might consider should be discussed with the company performing the work. You want to make sure that any modification that removes metal from your barrel can be performed without affecting the integrity of the metal.

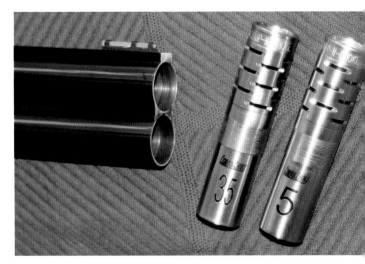

Some aftermarket chokes like these by Comp-n-Choke in Sylvania, Georgia, feature a wad stripping design that is said to stabilize and slow down the radical spin of the wad as it travels through the bore of the gun. This allows the shot charge to exit the shot cup and muzzle cleanly.

SHOTGUN CHOKES AND HOW THEY WORK

More than 100 years ago gunmakers and, to some extent, bird hunting aficionados blessed with mechanical and technical skills to work with metal began to experiment with ways to improve the downrange performance of their scatterguns. They did this by reducing the size of the bore diameter at the muzzle. The process was called choking, and many historians credit the great Illinois duck hunter Fred Kimble with developing the process. There is some question about the validity of these claims, since there are numerous accounts report such barrel experimentation years before Kimble's time. The first patent for shotgun chokes was filed by an American named Sylvester Roper. Ironically the Roper choke was well ahead of its time, since it was of the screw-in variety.

Regardless of where the practice of controlling shotgun patterns got started, chokes and choke systems have come a long way in their development since those early days. Today's wingshooters have the most advanced products ever developed at their disposal, but most hunters really don't understand what makes a choke perform the way it does.

There is more to how a gun patterns than just reducing the diameter of the barrel at the muzzle. The pressure that the ignited powder places on the wad and subsequently the shot charge as it exits the gun is a big factor in performance, as is the air resistance or drag once the pellets hit atmospheric resistance and the wad falls away from them. All of these factors contribute to how a gun performs since the difference in the width of a full choke and an improved cylinder choke is smaller than the diameter of a number nine shot pellet.

Let's take wad pressure and air resistance out of the performance equation for a moment and look at the choke itself and how it is configured in the barrel. First of all, in order for a choke to be effective, the transition between the bore diameter of the gun and the entry or opening of the choke should be .004 of an inch or less. In other words, you want your bore diameter and the mouth of the choke you put in it to match as closely as possible. For instance, if the bore of your barrel is .728 and the opening of the choke is .720, you might not get the optimum performance from the choke that

These custom choke tubes by Rob Roberts Custom Gunworks in Batesville, Arkansas feature one inch parallel sections within the choke wall. Most factory tubes have a parallel choke section that measures one half to three quarters of an inch. The longer parallel section is said to offer more stability to the shot charge just before it exits the muzzle. You wouldn't think that one quarter of an inch would matter, but it does.

you desire. While that doesn't sound like much of a difference, the pattern can be affected since the shot will encounter a transition difference of .008 in the bore versus the size of the mouth of the choke. Obviously this difference can cause increased pellet deformation and could cause barrel damage with high pressure loads or large shot sizes.

When the bore diameter of the barrel and the mouth of the choke are properly matched, the transition of the load into the choke itself will be fairly smooth. This will lessen the amount of pellet deformation as the load is squeezed into the smaller diameter of the choke, and will result in improved patterning performance.

If the transition into the choke is gentle, the length of the parallel section of the choke will help determine the long range performance characteristics of the barrel, choke and load combination. Many of the parallel sections in a factory choke tube are three quarters of an inch to an inch long. It is generally accepted that the longer and gentler the taper and parallel sections in a choke tube

There are slight, but meaningful differences between factory tubes and those manufactured by aftermarket companies. In most cases the difference is the bore/choke diameter match and a longer parallel section in the aftermarket choke.

are, the better overall performance they will have.

In recent years, aftermarket choke tubes have become readily available for guns with interchangeable systems. Many of these choke companies offer replacement tubes, which means that they are made to a standard bore opening that would typically be found in that model gun. The thread patterns are matched so they will screw in the gun just like the factory tubes.

Other companies take the aftermarket tube production a bit further by offering tubes that are custom built to exactly the dimensions of the individual barrel. These tubes tend to be a bit better in terms of performance since they are built to very exacting tolerances. In order to get the perfect match, the bore diameter will have to be measured with a bore micrometer. This can be

done by a gunsmith, the company providing the choke or by the gun owner if he has access to such a tool.

One advantage of the aftermarket tubes is that they are available for very specific types of shooting. For example, there are chokes made for everything from turkey hunting to waterfowl with steel shot. For shooters who are serious about their wingshooting, a closer look at the high tech world of choking might be beneficial.

PATTERNING FOR OPTIMUM PERFORMANCE

Certainly one of the more simple ways to evaluate shotgun performance is to shoot patterns to determine how and where the gun shoots with a particular choke and load. Shooting such patterns can be of significant value to a wingshooter, because he must have some indication of performance in order to make educated decisions on what to shoot under a variety of hunting conditions.

There are a number of ways that a wingshooter can pattern his gun to determine its optimum performance levels. The first type of patterning he can do is called point of impact. This allows him to check the impact point of the shot charge when the gun is properly mounted. This is best accomplished from a bench rest position and at relatively short range 20 to 25 yards, with tight chokes. In this instance, you can actually aim the gun.

Using a modified or tighter choke, shoot at pattern board or similar object with a desired impact point highlighted in the center of the desired target. Fire at least three shells at the target, and then check the points of impact relative to the aiming point. This will give the shooter some idea of whether or not the gun shoots exactly where it is pointed. This is one of the few times a wingshooter will ever actually aim a shotgun.

Another form of patterning is to shoot various chokes and loads at a stationary pattern board or sheet in order to determine what combination of the two works best in a particular gun. Perhaps the most important point that a shooter should remember here is that the patterns he shoots should

(left) Point of impact patterns are used to ensure a proper gun fit and mount. Place a target mark on a pattern plate or board, stand 16 yards from the target with the muzzle on a line to the target and the gun under the armpit. Push to the target and lift the gun to the face with a proper mount. When the gun comes to the face, pull the trigger.

(right) The result of the shot should put the pattern horizontally and vertically where you want the gun to shoot. This is very helpful for determining gun fit and perfecting gun mounts. Once you get the mount and fit dialed in, you should be able to place the shot on the pattern board the same way regardless of distance.

be shot at the distance he would intend to take his shots in the field. If most of his shots, for instance, will be taken at 30 yards, it will be all right to pattern at 40 yards as the industry standards suggest, but you might want to pattern test at 30 yards as well. You want to know what your gun will do at that 30-yard distance since that's the distance you'll be shooting most often.

This type of patterning is another situation where the shooter will aim the gun, because he is looking to center the pattern at a specific point on a stationary target. Even though the target is not moving, this exercise will allow the shooter to find the choke and load that shoots the most consistent

patterns in his gun at a prescribed distance. And by finding that level of optimum performance, the shooter can help dictate the success or failure for a day afield.

Most patterning is done by shooting at a 30 inch circle drawn on a pattern board or piece of paper. If using paper for a target, it's best to get as large a piece as possible. Forty two inch rolls of paper are available in most areas. Within the 30 inch circle, center a second circle that is 20 inches in diameter and add a third circle inside the 20 inch ring that is 10 inches in diameter. The outer ring will actually have a bit more surface area than the 20 inch inner circle, and when evaluating patterns, the concentration should be on the number of pellets in the 10 inch center core and 20 inch area.

Many shooters put real stock in the total number of pellet hits in the overall 30 inch ring, but those found in the outer ring will typically result in more crippled birds. The focus has to be on the performance in the center core, because those outer hits will ultimately be falling away from the shot string as they move towards the bird.

Ideally a wingshooter wants to see patterns that exceed 70 percent in the 30-inch circle, with the majority of the hits landing within the 20 inch core. If the pattern performance falls below the 70 percent density level, the choke should be tightened until that level is reached. If the performance indicates that the patterns are extremely tight, say in excess of 90 percent, perhaps a bit more open choke would be in order. Goose and tur-

key hunters, of course, relish 90 percent plus patterns, since the size of their quarry demands multiple pellet hits in lethal areas for a clean harvest.

To get a percentage reading on performance, divide the total number of hits by the average total number of pellets in the selected load. Don't count fringe hits and only use pellets clearly inside the circle to compute the average.

When analyzing the pattern, look for areas where holes are apparent. If there are noticeable deficiencies where holes of five or more inches without a hit in the pattern occur, either tighten the choke or change the load until the problem no longer exists. There are companies that specialize in fine tuning a barrel and choke combination, so if you can't get your gun to perform to your satisfaction, some professional assistance might help.

Wingshooters who prefer to hunt with smaller

Most shooters are concerned with a 30 inch pattern, but the meat of the pattern is found inside of the 20 inch ring. Hunters will want to select a choke and load that will give them optimum performance within the 20 inch circle at the distance they plan to shoot most of their birds.

Want to know how your gun performs with a certain choke and load? There's only one way.

gauges will find that the center density performance of their chosen gauge can be impressive. Unfortunately, the number of pellet hits in the annular ring will leave something to be desired as the chosen gauge gets smaller. So while it is a thrill to hunt gamebirds with the small gauges, hunters should realize that they are forcing themselves to be more precise with the handling of the gun and lead pictures when in the field.

An additional factor to consider is that the small gauge guns typically weigh quite a bit less than a 12 or 20 gauge of the same model. The very lightest and most difficult to control is the .410, and hunters who feel that they must shoot the

12 gauge through .410 patterns using standard hunting loads and #8 shot.

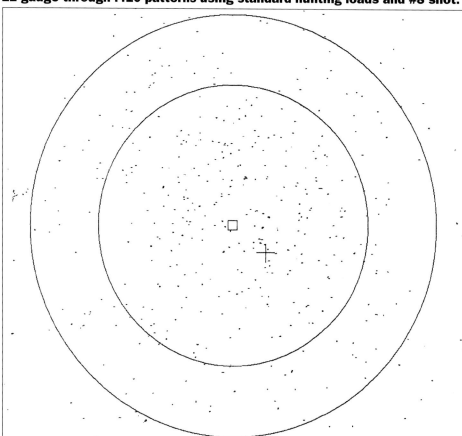

Firearm:
Winchester SX2

Choke mfr:
Rob Roberts Custom

Constriction:
Mod

Barrel selected:
S26

Cartridge Tested:
Winchester 1.125
8 SuperSPort 1300

Pellets in load: 461

Choke %: 85

30in Pellets: 392

20in Pellets: 265

10in Pellets: 93

**True Turkey
Factor:** 171

+ is the center of Red Dot.
Small square is the center
of your pattern.

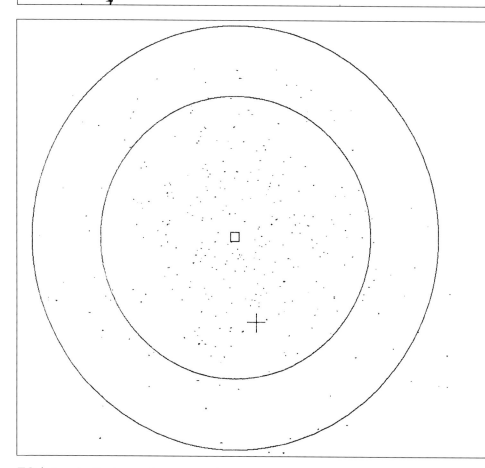

Firearm:
Remington 1100

Choke mfr:
Rob Roberts Custom

Constriction:
Mod

Barrel selected:
S26

Cartridge Tested:
Winchester 20
0.875 8 AA 1200

Pellets in load: 359

Choke %: 85.2

30in Pellets: 306

20in Pellets: 249

10in Pellets: 113

**True Turkey
Factor:** 169

+ is the center of Red Dot.
Small square is the center
of your pattern.

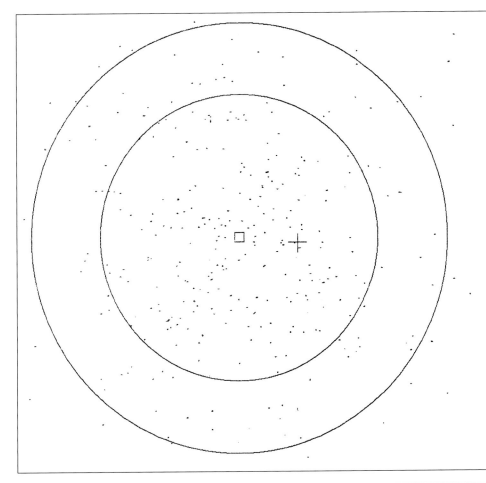

Firearm:
Remington 1100

Choke mfr:
Rob Roberts Custom

Constriction:
Mod

Barrel selected:
S26

Cartridge Tested:
Estate 28 0.75
8 SuperSport 1200

Pellets in load: 307

Choke %: 94.8

30in Pellets: 291

20in Pellets: 214

10in Pellets: 84

True Turkey Factor: 168

+ is the center of Red Dot.
Small square is the center
of your pattern.

small gauges might find significantly more success just by moving to a more weight and performance friendly 28 gauge gun.

Don't get caught up in shooting the smaller gauges because you think it is more sporting and gives the birds a chance. Fringe hits on a bird, unless the pellets strike a lethal area, simply result in a cripple, which may or may not be retrieved. Make sure that you use enough gun and the right load to match your shooting ability, because when live game is involved, there is no room for an overzealous ego.

This pattern was shot by the author in preparation for dove season. The 35 yard shot using a modified choke and a Winchester AA Heavy Target 7 ½ load placed the majority of the pellets within all four quadrants of the 20 inch ring. If the shot is properly centered, a bird would most likely be cleanly harvested.

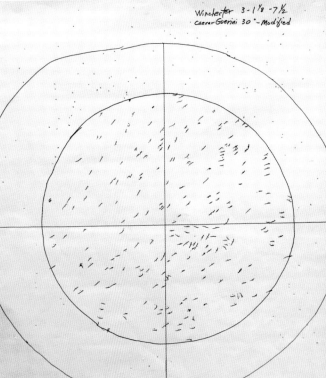

Winchester 3-1⅛ -7½
Caesar Guerini 30"-Modified

BEWARE THE AMMO YOU CHOOSE

Shooters will find significant differences in the performance characteristics of various loads. Promotional loads and other inexpensive ammunition will typically deliver poorer patterns, and only premium quality loads will give a true reading of the capabilities of a specific barrel and choke. Keep in mind, too, that a lower velocity load will usually deliver tighter patterns than one with a higher velocity.

It's also important to recognize that magnum loads don't necessarily throw a shot charge any faster or farther than a standard shot shell. They typically just put more shot in the pattern. As a result, they will sometimes provide killing patterns at slightly greater ranges, even though the downrange velocities are lower than in lighter weight charges. Finding a combination of adequate shot weight and velocity to match what's needed to cleanly harvest a given gamebird at a chosen distance will serve the needs of most shooters.

When patterning steel shot, the shooter will generally find that good center density is common. This can explain why many hunters are turned off by steel shot. Chances are pretty good that the tightness of the patterns are such that many shooter's skills are not equal to a load's perfor-

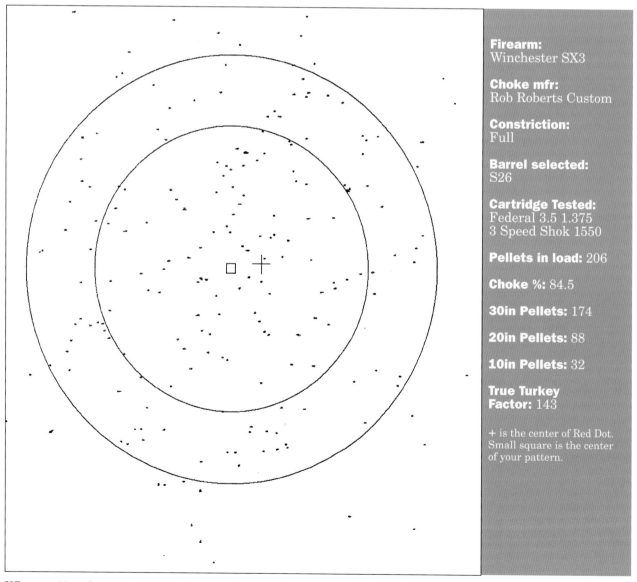

Firearm:
Winchester SX3

Choke mfr:
Rob Roberts Custom

Constriction:
Full

Barrel selected:
S26

Cartridge Tested:
Federal 3.5 1.375
3 Speed Shok 1550

Pellets in load: 206

Choke %: 84.5

30in Pellets: 174

20in Pellets: 88

10in Pellets: 32

True Turkey Factor: 143

+ is the center of Red Dot. Small square is the center of your pattern.

When patterning steel loads, look to get most of your pellets within that 20 inch ring.

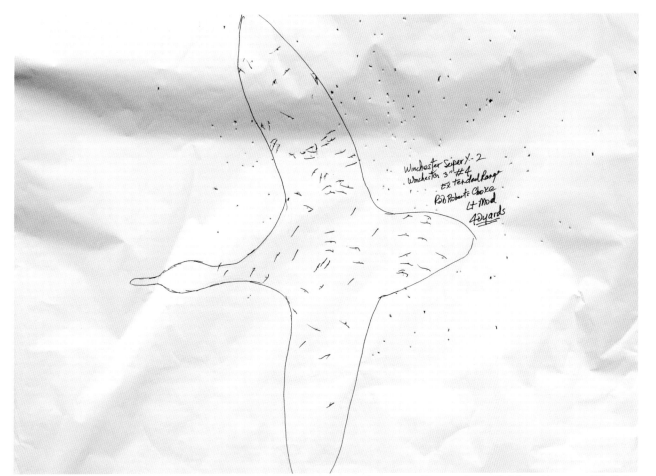

Handwritten on pattern: Winchester Super X-2
Winchester 3" #4
Extended Range
Rob Roberts Choke
Lt Mod
40 yards

Tungsten based loads tend to be heavier than lead, and they usually produce tight patterns with fairly open chokes. This pattern was shot with Winchester Extended Range #4 waterfowl loads through a light modified choke tube.

mance capabilities. Many birds are hit with the outer fringe of a pattern, or are missed altogether with such tight shooting loads.

Some wingshooters take patterning a bit farther by actually drawing the outline of the bird they are testing for in the center of the circle and in other areas within it as well. This can be an eye opening experience, especially when the shooter examines the number of lethal hits in the bird's outline. Regardless of which type of patterning is used, it is important to shoot a least five shots to get an average of overall performance.

Choosing the right choke and load combination for a selected type of game bird is a critical element to the success of the hunt, and finding the optimum performance level of a particular scattergun is a major part of the outdoor experience.

When patterning for wingshooting, try drawing an outline of the bird(s) you'll be hunting on the pattern sheet to better determine the effectiveness of your choke/load combination. This diagram was copied from a mounted pintail drake (tail left off intentionally).

The Principles
of Gun Mount

Getting set up early for a shot in the field can really help the gun mount and insertion point.

It's pretty common for wingshooters to become frustrated when they miss birds consistently. Unfortunately it doesn't matter how many dollars they invest in equipment and modifications to their guns to make them shoot their best if they can't bring the gun properly to the face and shoulder as the gun is mounted. If the shooter cannot make a proper mount before the lead picture develops, a miss is certain to follow.

A common statement used by many shooting instructors use is "its not the arrow, it's the Indian." And frankly, if the gun fits the shooter properly and the right choke and load has been selected,

that statement is right on. A similar analogy can be made using the popular game of golf as a subject. No matter how fancy and expensive a set of golf clubs is, if the face of the club doesn't strike the ball properly, an errant shot will always be the result.

Wingshooting is no different. With the gun fitted properly, a successful shot is always dependent on a precise gun mount, since the rear sight on the shotgun is the eye on the side of the shooting shoulder. Gun mounts are typically easier to master in a controlled environment like a sporting clays course or trap or skeet field because the

Shooter with proper preshot style and position.

target presentations are known. But in a true field situation with the possibility of an unpredictable bird presenting itself in a variety of ways, solid gun mounts are just as critical, but often more difficult for shooters to physically master consistently.

Perhaps the most graphic picture one can visualize when it comes to poor gun mounts is the color of a shooter's shoulder at the end of a good dove shoot. Most of the time, dove seasons start around the first of September. And for the hunter who doesn't shoot clays or travel south of the equator to shoot birds, a day in a dove field is often the first time he will use his shotgun following a few months of inactivity.

In many states dove hunters shoot in lightweight shirts early in the season, and the recoil from a box or two of shells can take its toll on the shoulder if the mounts aren't perfect. When the gun mount is missed because of poor mechanics, the butt of the stock can land just about anywhere. And when that spot is not in the pocket of the shoulder where it should be, a bruise is almost certain to occur. When you compound missed gun mounts over a number of shots, it is easy to see where the black and blue marks come from. And when you consider that the mount has to be correct every time, it is easy to see why it is such a key element of every shot.

Mounting a shotgun properly is a matter of eye and hand mechanics, where the hands work in tandem to bring the eyes or rear sight in line with the front sight or muzzle of the gun at a specific spot relative to the target. This has to be executed with the least amount of effort and wasted movement. To do this consistently, an understanding of how to hold the gun and how to master the movement required to bring the gun to the face are required.

Correct hand position on the stock and forearm are critical elements of the mounting process. First of all the trigger hand should hold the grip comfortably, not too tight or too loose. A grip that is too tight will impede the forearm hand from steering the gun. It will also slow down the consistency of the mount, and could cause a flinch or a noticeable

dip in the muzzle as the gun is brought to the face. On the other hand, holding the grip too loose can cause the shooter to lose control of the mount.

Therefore, the trigger hand should be positioned on the grip as if you were shaking hands with a friend. The thumb should not stay on top of the grip, rather it should be rolled over comfortably to further stabilize the grip. A thumb that remains on top of the stock could cause it to impede the sight picture down the gun or impact the face from the felt recoil of the shot, both of which could cause the face to lift off the stock.

The trigger should be pulled with the fleshy part of the index finger. This is the part of the finger that gives you the best feel and control of the trigger pull. And the trigger should be squeezed, not jerked.

There are a couple of ways to position the fore-

Leaving the thumb on top of the grip can lead to problems.

A proper grip is similar to shaking hands. The thumb should be rolled over the grip.

arm hand on the gun. Since so much of shotgunning is essentially like pointing your finger, some shooters like to place the hand on the forearm with the index finger pointing straight down the barrel. It is theorized that by pointing the finger where the gun looks, getting the gun to the target line and obtaining the right lead should be more natural.

The other commonly used style of hand positioning on the forearm is to simply cradle the gun in the palm of the hand so that it has a controlling feel for the shooter. In either case, the hand should not grip the forearm too tightly. As with the trigger hand, a comfortable grip on the forearm will produce better results.

The forearm hand can be too close to the receiver or too far out. Either one can affect the mount and balance of the gun.

When the forearm hand is properly positioned, the gun will flow to the target and face more smoothly.

When presented with a driven vertical shot, the forearm hand can be moved slightly closer to the receiver, which will give you more vertical swing radius.

Many wingshooters got their shooting start with a rifle, so they might want to hold a shotgun like they might a rifle by resting the forearm of the shotgun on top of the thumb and index finger. This hand position really puts the shooter at a disadvantage, because he has limited his control of the gun and placed more control and steering on the trigger hand. Remember that the gun should be held comfortably and firmly so as to allow the hands to move the stock to the face and the muzzle to the bird.

Another factor that contributes to good gun mounts is where the forearm hand is positioned on the gun. Most shooters will find that when the gun length is proper for them, the forearm hand can be positioned near the center of the forearm.

If the hand is too far forward, chances are that it will impede the gun from mounting properly. In fact, the gun will feel too long for the shooter, and the chances of snagging the heel of the stock on a piece of clothing are increased. Get the hand too far back and towards the receiver and the balance of the gun can be affected. With the hand too far back, the muzzle of the gun can easily dip as it is being mounted, which greatly affects the control of the swing and subsequent lead picture.

One way to determine where the hand should be placed on the forearm is to point the gun straight up with the gun being held by the trigger hand only. Since this is the most arm extension that a shooter will ever have when taking a shot, he should comfortably reach up with his forearm hand and grip the gun without having to extend his arm. By placing the hand in this spot, the shooter should be able to crisply mount the gun with minimal muzzle movement.

Once the hands are correctly and comfortably placed on the gun, the mechanics of getting the gun to the face are made easier, but in order to master the gun mount for wingshooting, the hands must work as a team. In most instances, hunters who have trouble with the mount do so because they exert more pressure with their trigger hand than with the forearm hand. This is not surprising, however, since the trigger hand is typically the strongest and most used hand in other activities.

When the trigger hand overpowers the forearm hand, the muzzle tends to move vertically first before it moves to the line of the bird. Unfortunately the gun cannot move horizontally and vertically at the same time, so the shooter loses time and distance on the bird because of the unnecessary movement of the muzzle.

To correctly mount a shotgun when wingshooting, the shooter should push his forearm hand to where he wants to insert the gun relative to his target as it comes to his face. This push initiates the mount, which is completed as the trigger hand simply lifts the stock to the face. The push and lift should utilize the same force with each hand so that there is no discernible dip or wiggle of the muzzle.

It should be noted that in wingshooting, the gun is steered to the target and target line with the forearm hand. This will get the gun in position for a shot much more quickly than trying to move to the bird with the trigger hand and/or body. Shooters should avoid mounting the gun and then taking it to the target. This is called "boxing the bird," which is a good description for a two move mount. The proper gun mount requires only one move to the bird with the front hand.

As the gun is mounted on most shots, the shooter's weight will generally shift from his back foot to his front foot in order to counterbalance the added weight of the muzzle over the front foot. The only exception to this balance shift would be on birds whose flight path is below the shooter's feet or on high overhead driven birds. In the instance where the target is below the shooter's feet, the weight should start more on the front foot if possible, which will minimize any vertical travel of the gun. On the other hand, a driven target is best taken with the weight shifting primarily from the front foot to the back foot as the gun is brought overhead. On driven birds it is also important to position the feet a bit closer together to allow a fluid vertical movement with the gun. A wide stance in this situation will impede the shooters ability to move the gun to the vertical position and beyond.

When shooting driven birds, the arms will be

(right) When the feet are out of place on an overhead shot, it is difficult to move the gun smoothly through the kill zone.

(far right) Weight transfer and balance are critical to making overhead shots consistently.

fully extended on shots taken directly overhead. In addition to the weight shift to the back foot, the forearm hand can be moved slightly closer to the receiver to give the shooter the additional arm extension needed for such a shot.

Good gun mounts are a product of solid, consistent mechanics. When a shooter misses his mount, he generally knows it, as the sight picture he is accustomed to is suddenly changed. Unfortunately it is virtually impossible to quickly modify the mount because as the bird continues its flight because the required sight picture for a successful shot is constantly changing.

The reasons for mount problems are varied, but they usually stem from one of these factors: 1) the shooter was surprised by the appearance of the bird and rushed to mount the gun; 2) he was walking and was therefore out of position to move the gun to the bird; or 3) there were flaws in how both hands moved the gun through the mount process.

When you're out of position for a shot, the mount can be adversely affected.

Perhaps the most important thing for a wing-shooter to remember is that he usually has more time to take a shot than he thinks. As a result, executing the mechanics of a solid mount will give a hunter a timing edge over a speeding bird, since the gun gets into position to take the shot more quickly.

PERFECTING THE MOUNT WITH PRACTICE

Fortunately the gun mount can be perfected by practice. As with other sports, your gun mount mechanics and technique can be constantly improved by training the muscles to position the gun in the same place every time. There are some exercises that you can do to develop the muscle memory to mount the gun on command every time.

First of all, check the gun to make sure it is not loaded, and check to make sure that the direction you wish to point it is safe. Then position yourself in front of a mirror and practice the mount using your nose in that mirror as a target. Start with the muzzle just below the nose so that as you push to it with your forearm hand and lift the gun to the face, it will mount right on the target line. This visual picture that you see in the mirror will help you to control the muzzle better. You will be able to notice any discernible dip or unnecessary movement of the barrel, and you will be able to improve the consistency of your mount.

Perform this exercise until you reach muscle fatigue. Initially sets of 25 will be about right. You will find that you can do more and more reps each time as the muscles build. But the real advantage to gun mount practice is the developed motor skills that will help get the gun in position in the field more quickly.

Once the mount mechanics become automatic, you can practice mounting and moving the gun laterally. Again making sure the gun is unloaded, find a safe area in your home where the ceiling and a wall intersect. There will be a definable line where the two meet. Using this line as the line of a bird, move and mount the gun along that line as if tracking a bird in flight.

There are aftermarket products that can be inserted inside of the muzzle that will project a beam of light onto the wall which indicate where the gun would shoot if the trigger were pulled. One very inexpensive product that can be used is a MagLite that takes AA batteries. This sized light will fit snugly into a 12 gauge gun with a modified choke tube installed. With the light turned to its smallest spot, it will give you a good picture of whether or not you and the gun are looking at the same location, and will certainly show you any unnecessary movement of the gun as it is being mounted and swung. When doing this exercise, keep this one thing in mind. Everywhere the gun goes, the light goes. So if the mount and swing are not smooth when doing this exercise, they won't be smooth in the field either.

By being able to properly mount the gun every time the hunter can greatly improve his chances of making a successful shot in the field. Missing the mount can only increase his stress, since failure to line up the front and rear sights on a shotgun usually result in a miss. And keep in mind that practice makes perfect.

Some of the best and least expensive practice is gun mounts with a safe gun and mirror.

A AA-sized Mag-Lite fits perfectly in a 12 gauge modified choke, and you can define gun mounts and insertion points at home.

Understanding Proper Foot and Body Position

Once a wingshooter has mastered the mechanics of the gun mount and swing, he will find that his shot making ability improves significantly as long as he is able to swing and follow through after the shot is fired. To do this consistently, the position of the shooter's feet and body have to be properly aligned if the shot sequence is to take place comfortably.

With lots of practice, you'll be ready when the time comes to make that perfect shot.

Many wingshooters miss birds because they find themselves physically out of position when the target presents itself for a shot. And since shooters are often walking behind dogs when afield, it's pretty easy to be caught in mid-stride

(far left) If your stance is too open, your body movement will be compromised.

(left) With your feet set properly, moving the gun through the shot zone and follow though are much easier.

or on the wrong foot when the target is first visible. So let's look at some of the inherent problems encountered while shooting in the field. With the problems identified, we can discuss ways to make sure the feet and body are in the proper position when it's time to shoot.

We can begin with foot position, because how the feet are placed will determine whether or not the shooter will be able to make a complete swing and follow through as a shot is being taken. There are a number of shooting stances that are recognized in wingshooting circles around the world. Some of them (Stanbury method) recommend that the feet stay positioned close together to allow a smooth, fluid transfer of the gun to the shoulder, target and lead picture. Other styles suggest that the feet be more spread apart (Churchill method). (These styles will be further discussed in Chapter Nine.)

Regardless of the shooting stance used, if the feet of a right handed shooter are too closed at the firing point, the shooter will usually miss behind the bird because he will start to run out of swing radius before the shot and follow through can be completed. If his stance is too open, he could miss in front since it's possible for the gun to come to the face too far in front of the bird, thereby disrupting the timing of the swing sequence.

The best foot position is that which is employed by many sporting clays shooters around the world. Of course, they have the luxury of knowing precisely where their target will fly, so getting setup for a shot is pretty easy. Experienced wingshooters can predict where they plan to shoot at a speeding bird once they identify its speed, angle and distance. As a result, they get in position to take the shot more quickly and never appear to be rushed.

(far left) Left handed shooters should point their right foot in the direction of the shot zone.

(left) Many shooters with a slender physique prefer more of a rifle stance.

For right handed shooters, the feet should not be too far apart and the left foot should typically be pointed slightly ahead of where they plan to pull the trigger. The reason for this is to counterbalance the added weight of the gun in front of the body. By slightly bending the left leg at the knee, while keeping the right leg fairly straight, the shooter's balance will remain intact as he moves through the swing radius of the shot. This can be accomplished by anticipating the angle and line of the bird, and simply stepping with the front foot towards that spot. For the left hand shooter, the above scenario is reversed.

When it comes to foot position, it is most important for the shooter to be comfortable and balanced as the gun is coming to the face. If the mount and swing feels funny, chances are that the feet are out of position to make the shot. Remember that if there is a balance problem for the shooter as he is completing his swing, the gun may not be able to finish with a good follow through. In most cases, this is a result of poor foot position.

The shooter will have more control of his swing if he stands more squarely to the target. Somewhere in the neighborhood of 45 degrees to the kill zone is best for most shooters. This is important because it allows the shooting shoulder to come into the gun as it is being brought to the face. Shooters who take more of a rifle stance approach will have to bring the gun back to the shoulder when mounting and in many instances will wind up with the gun more on the biceps of the arm than in the shoulder pocket. This could explain many of the gun induced bruises on many shooters after a day of shooting.

The physical makeup of the shooter has something to do with how he squares to the target for a shot. Shooters with a slender physique tend to stand at that aforementioned 45-degree angle

Understanding Proper Foot and Body Position | **93**

to the shot as the gun is mounted and the shot taken. Guns with a more pronounced physique and a wider face tend to stand more squarely to the target. In both cases, it is important to position the feet before the gun is completely mounted so that the swing and follow through may take place unhindered.

Keep in mind that in wingshooting the gun is steered to the target with the forearm hand and arm. But if you go to a trap and skeet club, you will most likely see shooters with the gun pre-mounted on the shoulder prior to the target being visible. In sporting clays and hunting, the gun has to be led to the target from a much lower position

Big bodied shooters often require a more open stance because of their wide shoulders and facial features.

Shooting with the wrong foot forward not only looks awkward, it feels awkward too.

when the gun starts from off the shoulder.

The key to this point is that since the arms lead the gun, it is critical for the feet to be in position just ahead of where the shot will be taken so the arms and body can complete the move to the and forward of the bird without running out of swing. In many instances, the shooter can get the gun to the bird if his feet are set up behind the shot zone, but he will find it difficult to get the muzzle ahead of the bird and to the desired lead.

GETTING SET WHILE ON THE MOVE

As discussed earlier, in many types of wing-shooting, the hunter is on foot and moving either to flush a bird that has been located by a gun dog or one that will be pushed skyward by his forward movement. When this is the case, the hunter must locate the bird visually and determine its speed, angle and distance so that the feet and body can be positioned immediately toward the spot where

As you move in on a pointing dog, remember that you have time to step in the direction of the shot as the gun is being mounted.

the shot will be taken.

This will happen most often when the front foot has been properly placed at or just ahead of the desired shooting point. When a bird presents itself to the shooter, he must be cognizant of the amount of time he has to get positioned before squeezing the trigger. If the front foot moves quickly to the shooting zone, a good mount, insertion point relative to the bird and swing will almost always lead to a successful shot. The key to a successful shot execution here is to set the feet either before or during the move to the bird. The more you work on this, the easier it will be to perform consistently.

with each of these dog types.

The pointing dog is trained to locate birds and hold point on them until the hunter or dog handler moves in to flush the birds. Under no circumstances should the dog flush the birds unless he is released to do so.

There are some tell tale signs offered by pointing breeds as they locate and point their quarry. Most of the time hunters can tell when their dogs are "birdy," as the demeanor of the animal changes as a bird is scented. Their activity becomes more deliberate, and once the bird's scent is detected the dog will go on point to identify its location. If the dog is not sure of the bird's whereabouts, it will relocate until it pinpoints where the bird is.

Seasoned hunters can read the dog's body language and tell whether or not it has the bird located. The eyes, head position and tail of the animal tell the experienced gun where the bird is, and here's what they look for.

In virtually all instances the dog's tail will be wagging as it locates the bird. Once the bird is exactly located, however, the tail will become stationary. It's not uncommon for the dog's body to be facing one direction and its head yet another. Look at the direction where the dog's head is facing and look at the concentration in its eyes. Its tail should be locked and motionless. This should be a sign that the dog has determined the precise location of the bird.

Once the point is established, the hunter should scan the area around the dog to find areas that might hold the bird. You should also look at the background to determine the safe shot zones and to determine where you think the bird might fly. Remember that the dog will generally be downwind of the bird, and that birds tend to take off into the wind.

When a dog goes on point, it is critical for the hunter to get to the dog quickly, especially when hunting wild birds. When the birds flush, make sure that they get high enough before taking a shot. No matter how steady a bird dog might be, there's always the chance that the excitement of a flush will cause him to leap upward at the birds.

HUNTING WITH A POINTING OR FLUSHING DOG

As mentioned earlier, many upland gunners hunt with their choice of "man's best friend." There are two types of dogs used in the uplands: pointing dogs and flushing dogs. You'll find that there is a significant difference in how you hunt

When hunting with a flushing like this Labrador Retriever, you will find yourself moving and working with the dog as it quarters back in forth in front of your constantly moving position.

If you don't see your flushing target against the horizon, it's best not to take the shot.

Flushing dogs are different animals all together. Their job is to constantly move and locate the birds. They are not trained to hold point until the hunter gets to them, so it's important to work a flushing dog well within gun range of the hunter.

Since they will not hold point until the hunter gets in position, it is critical to work with the dog by moving with it as it hunts. The trained flushing dog will work in a quartering fashion in front of the guns, and once it scents a bird, its pace will increase. The tail moves more quickly and there is a more determined demeanor about the dog.

When a flushing dog indicates that it has found scent, hunters need to get ready. With the dog in

constant motion pressuring the birds, they are likely on the move and could flush at any time. Once again the experienced gun will be able to look around his immediate area to determine where the birds might be and where his safe shooting lanes are. The dog should be working into the wind, and the birds should flush into the wind as well.

Once the birds flush, the eyes of the hunter focus on the bird to be shot. As the gun mount commences, the front foot steps toward the intended shot position. Once this is done in the mere seconds it takes, the gun can comfortably move into position to harvest the bird. The most important part of the shot sequence is to focus on your target first. Once the eyes lock on a bird, the rest of the sequence will naturally occur.

When shooting from a layout blind, this is often the view you will have when covered up.

SHOOTING FROM A SEATED OR LAYING POSITION

Waterfowl hunters often find themselves having to shoot landing or passing birds from a seated or laying position. The dove hunter spends much of his day afield sitting on a stool or chair, and many of his shots are taken from the seated position as well. These types of shots can be quite demanding since the body tends to be in an awkward state for a shot if certain adjustments aren't made.

From the seated position, getting set to take a

shot is similar to doing so while on foot. The shooter will have plenty of time if he visually locates the bird and positions the trunk of his body so that, when the shot is taken, he can move the gun through that shot window comfortably.

He can do this by simply moving the feet left or right as is required. Again, getting the body in position quickly will give him a much better chance for success. This allows the gun to travel its full course relative to the flight path of the bird.

Remember that there is almost always more time than the shooter thinks, even from this position. It is the initial positioning of the body that will allow the completion of the shot that counts.

When a shooter is lying down, such as in the middle of a spread of goose decoys, he must first get himself in position to mount and swing the gun before he can execute the shot. In many instances he will be watching a particular bird that he has chosen as his target. With the bird in view, the shooter can either sit up or get to his knees, position himself comfortably and still get a shot off. All of this is predicated on the shooter not getting in too much of a hurry. Again, time is usually on the side of the shooter.

If a specific bird has not been selected as a target, he will still find that he has time to execute a shot if there is no wasted motion. The key, however, is to make sure that the body is balanced before moving the gun to the bird.

Shots can also be taken from an on ground seated position. Again, balance is the key, so getting the body comfortably set before moving the gun to the bird can insure success. Most of time the shooter will be sitting up from a lay down position. This setup usually occurs when shooting from a coffin or pop up blind or when laying on the ground in a decoy spread.

As you come to the seated position, make sure you pick out your target first before mounting the gun. Once the target is sighted, moving the gun to the mount and insertion point will be much easier.

If you're shooting from a laying position, make sure you set your position before the mount takes place.

To shoot from a laying position, start by picking out your target as you are sitting up. The gun will come up with you and you will push the gun with the forearm hand to the desired insertion point to begin the shot sequence. Make sure that your blind is set to accommodate wind direction and whether you are right or left handed.

Without question foot and body position are key elements to making a good shot, since they allow the shooter to swing and follow through. And having the confidence that there is no need to rush as long as the feet and body are positioned just slightly ahead of where the shot will be taken. This will give the shooter a decided advantage to take one, two or even three shots comfortably.

Let's face it. Good gun fit and a proper gun mount are only beneficial if the shooter is able to move to the bird and the proper lead picture. Getting the body set properly before the shot is taken helps make this possible.

CHAPTER

8

Vision and Its Inherent Problems

There is no doubt that once a shooter learns to correctly mount and swing his shotgun the most important factor determining whether or not he hits his target is how he uses his vision to his advantage. Vision is defined as how we react to what the eyes see. You see, in shotgun shooting the eyes lead the hands to a moving target, just as they move the hands to catch a baseball or shoot a basket. Granted, the hands and arms do most of the physical work, but without the eyes as a steering mechanism, we would really have no chance of success with any of these things.

Consider that the vast majority of what we do physically is controlled by our vision. And since shooting requires motor skills that are fueled by what the eyes see, an understanding of this remarkable sense and some of the problems that are common to the wingshooting fraternity seem to be in order.

ONE EYE OR TWO?

Humans were blessed with binocular vision, meaning that both eyes are used together to send visual information to the brain. With both eyes open and focused, we are capable of seeing a visual field of approximately 180 degrees. With one eye closed that visual field is decreased to around 150 degrees or less. As a result, more visual information is transmitted to the brain with both eyes open than with one eye open.

Since most of us began our shooting with a .22 rifle, we were taught to aim at our target. With one eye closed we could line up the sights on that target and generally hit it if our aim was true. It's fair to say that most rifle shooting is at stationary targets, since hitting them if they were moving would be quite a challenge.

In wingshooting, the vast majority of shots are taken at birds in flight. These speedy targets tend to present the shooter with a wide variety of speeds, distances and angles. Because of the continuous changes in the flight path of those flying targets, it is helpful to have all of our visual skills to draw from. As a result, shotgun shooting is usually a two-eyed game, since both eyes open provide us with the maximum use of our peripheral vision and depth perception.

How much better are two eyes than one? Try this test and see what your results are. When riding as a passenger down the road and clear of any traffic obstacles, try closing one eye for a short time. Most people will feel an immediate sense of dizziness and a significant loss of focus on the road ahead. If this happens in driving, imagine how you would be affected when participating in other sports, like golf or tennis. Shooting is really no different when you examine how the eyes and hands must work together.

This is not to say that a shotgun can't be consistently used successfully by a shooter who uses just one eye. It most certainly can be. There are thousands of terrific shooters who are just deadly on birds with one eye closed or blocked in some manner, but imagine how much more they could see if they let both eyes work for them. Doesn't it make sense to take advantage of all of our vision rather than just half of it?

The majority of shooters who close an eye have a tendency to focus more on the gun than on the bird. As a result the gun leads the eyes rather than the eyes leading the hands and subsequently the gun. The eyes can be trained where to look, and when the shooter can depend on this peripheral vision, depth perception and ability to focus beyond the gun to the bird, his chances for a successful shot are significantly improved. Using both eyes to do this can only increase one's awareness of what is happening in front of the shooter.

WHAT SHOULD YOU SEE?

The very best wingshooters have the ability to see a picture that will break a target or bring down a speedy bird as they look through the beads on their gun. Notice the use of the words "through the beads." Many shooters don't fully understand what this means, so they spend time either aiming the gun or looking over it to see if they hit their target. Rest assured that when these things happen, the result with most often be a miss.

Whether you shoot with one eye or two, the picture through the gun should be about the same – that of a hard focus on the target and a soft focus on the gun. With both eyes open, you'll gather much more visual information because your peripheral vision will come into play.

The soft focus on the gun seems to be the toughest part of the shooting equation for many shooters. The best way to explain what that means is for you to point your shotgun at an object. Once pointed close the off eye and actually aim at the object. Once the aiming exercise is complete, open the other eye if you are a two eyed shooter and transfer the focus from the gun directly to the target. Once focused on the target, be aware of the muzzle without looking directly at it. You'll see a soft, fuzzy focus on the gun. You know exactly where it is, but you aren't looking at it. That's the picture. If you're shooting with one eye, the same exercise applies to you. Simply transfer the focus to the target while being aware of the muzzle. And once you have it, you'll have greater confidence when it comes to lead picture identification.

MAKING USE OF THE DOMINANT EYE

When a shooter looks down a gun with both eyes open, he should have an awareness of the gun as he looks straight down the barrel and focuses on his target. In some instances, however, he will see down the side of the barrel which can create a very confusing picture. If it appears that the sight picture is more across the barrel than straight down it, the shooter could have an eye dominance problem. The confusing picture across the barrel is known in the shooting world as cross firing or cross dominance.

Strangely enough, at the range that most of our shots in the field are taken, the eyes are equally dominant. This phenomenon occurs only within a few feet of the eyes, so when the gun is mounted right in front of them, the brain is forced to choose a dominant side.

With both eyes open, focus on an object, extend the hands in front of your face. Without adjusting the hands, position an object in the center of a small circle that you've made with your hands.

With the object centered, both eyes open and hands extended, simply bring the hands to the face, keeping the object in the center of the circle. The hands will come to the dominant eye.

You can also perform this dominance exercise using a piece of paper with a hole in the center.

With both eyes open, center an object in the hole and pull the paper to the face, keeping the object in the center of the hole. The hole will come to the dominant eye.

You see, each of us has a dominant eye that allows us to look directly down the barrel of the gun and out to the target with both eyes open. The dominant eye is not necessarily the eye that is the strongest in terms of visual acuity. Rather it is the eye which focuses on an object first as determined by the brain. This focus difference between the two eyes only takes a few milliseconds, but the brain determines which eye will focus first. Therefore it is possible for the weaker of the two eyes to be dominant.

There are a number of ways to determine which of your eyes is dominant. Here are two very simple methods that will help you determine your dominant eye.

First extend both hands straight out from your shoulders and bring them together in front of your nose. With the hands together, form a small hole so that you can see through it to a selected object in front of your face. With both eyes open center the object in the hole and bring the hands to the face with the object always remaining in the center of the hole. The hands will come to the master eye if you follow these steps.

A second method is to cut a small hole in the center of a piece of paper. Extend the arms in front of the face, and with both eyes open, center an object in the hole. With the eyes open bring the paper to the face, leaving the object in the center of the hole. The paper and hole will come to the dominant eye.

Assuming a proper gun fit and mount, the shooter will have no problem determining which eye is dominant, if the dominance is strong. The cross firing view down the rib with both eyes open will be a dead giveaway assuming a proper gun fit and mount.

For most shooters, this test will confirm that their dominant eye is on the same side as their shooting shoulder. But what about those shooters who are, for instance, right handed and test left eye dominant? Well, it's not the end of the world because there are remedies that will allow the eyes and gun to look at the same spot.

There are three ways that a shooter can compensate for an eye dominance problem. First of all, he can do what most wingshooters do when they have this problem. He can close the off eye, which will certainly place the shoulder side eye down the gun. This remedy, however, will still present the drawbacks discussed earlier.

A second remedy would be to patch his shooting glasses by blocking out the spot on the lens where the eye jumps across the gun. With both eyes open, this spot can be located by having a shooting partner move his index finger around the glasses lens of the off eye until the shoulder side eye is looking right down the rib of the gun. Using a small piece of Scotch tape, a small amount of Chapstick rubbed on the spot or a commercial product such as a MagicDot will do the job. The MagicDot is a product which allows the spot to be covered with a tape like substance that matches the color of the shooting glasses lens, the dominance jump can be blocked.

Some shooters cover the entire glasses lens of the off eye. While effective, the complete loss of the eye will significantly limit the shooter's ability to make use of his peripheral vision and depth perception. Full use of both eyes is hindered.

The third remedy is to simply change to the dominant eye shoulder. This will allow you to look down the gun properly with both eyes open, and will greatly improve your peripheral vision and depth perception. Without question, new shooters should start with the gun on the side of the dominant eye if they plan to be serious about their shooting. Keep in mind that the muscles must be trained to mount and swing the gun, regardless of which shoulder you choose to shoot from, so it would be best to train the hands and the dominant eye to work together.

Switching shoulders would be the best of these suggestions for the novice to beginner shooter. Since the muscles have to be trained for proper gun mount mechanics anyway, why not go into the excitement of wingshooting with both eyes open.

You will note that there is no suggestion of learning to shoot with a cross dominant condition when both eyes are open. The lead pictures that the shooter would need to see under these circumstances are so different and confusing than those experienced when looking right down the barrel

One way to offset a dominance problem is to position a piece of tape or Chapstick on your glasses exactly where the cross over point is for the dominant eye. Have the shooter focus down the gun with both eyes open. Move your finger around the lens of the off eye until the shooter is looking straight through the rib of the gun. That's where you dab a bit of Chapstick because that is where the dominance jump takes place.

that they would make learning to shoot this way very difficult. It's much better to get the shoulder side eye looking straight down the gun if you want to experience consistency.

Using these three remedies for eye dominance, shooters can also learn to cope with other problems such as center dominance, where neither eye proves to be dominant; the lack of ability to close an eye if needed; and vision where one eye is noticeably stronger in acuity than the other.

A fourth remedy is available, but not often used. There are companies who manufacture a

product known as a cross over stock. This stock is configured so that a right hand/left eye dominant shooter could mount the gun on his right shoulder, but have the sighting plane in front of the dominant left eye.

LEARN TO USE YOUR VISION

One of the problems facing many shooters is that they really don't know how to use their vision to help them get the muzzle of the gun properly positioned to take a shot. The best wing shots understand how to transfer their visual focus out to the target and beyond the gun, but for many shooters this can prove to be troublesome.

Professional shooting instructors will suggest that their students concentrate on their shot. What they are really suggesting is for the shooter to dial his focus more specifically to a visual center. In most instances the wingshooter's visual center is the leading edge or head of the bird. The better a shooter is at acquiring his visual center and holding it through the shot, the more success

Shooting a shotgun is very similar to pointing your finger. We all have that inherent ability.

he will have in the field.

Fortunately there is a way to practice this at home, so when the time comes to take a shot the eyes automatically focus on the target while sensing the muzzle position rather than it being the other way around. Here is an exercise that might help if you are having problems focusing ahead of the gun to the bird.

If you want to train the eyes to focus on the target, set up a scenario where they are required to focus in order to get results. When practicing your gun mounts at home, try pointing at objects that you can read words or numbers from. For instance, try pointing at calendars, clocks, posters, etc. or place a newspaper or magazine against a wall and try reading the large print from a distance as the gun is mounted. This will help you shift your focus to the target only. Of course, you should make sure that the muzzle always points in a safe direction when performing this or any exercise with your gun.

EYE FATIGUE – THE WINGSHOOTER'S NEMESIS

Even the best of shooters find themselves in a struggle with success in the field when their eyes are strained and tired. It is difficult to maintain your visual center when the eyes feel stress. Eye exercises to strengthen the eye muscles and proper shooting glass colors that help offer a contrast between the bird and the background while relaxing the eyes will help fend off eye fatigue.

In some instances eye fatigue will cause the shooter to think that his eyes are changing dominance. Chances are that the dominant eye is asking for more help from the off eye due to fatigue setting in because of bright sun, low light or lots of shooting. Keep in mind that the more you work the eyes, the more they depend on each other to feed information to the brain.

Interchangeable lens colors can be very helpful as light and background changes.

CHANGING EYE DOMINANCE

If shooting from the dominant eye side is so very important, can a shooter shift his dominance to his dominant physical side if there is a problem? There are many trains of thought regarding this issue, but it is questionable as to whether or not dominance can in fact be completely changed.

There are theories that indicate that intense focus exercises will help shift the dominance over, as might keeping the dominant eye closed to create a dependence on the other eye, which could help strengthen it. In some instances, these theories might work, but most shooters aren't willing to commit the exercise time required to take the chance.

So if eye dominance appears to be a problem, it's probably best to work through it using one of the three suggestions discussed earlier.

THE VALUE OF SHOOTING GLASSES

You can't go to a shooting range these days without having to wear some kind of eye protection. There are obvious reasons for wearing shooting glasses or glasses with lenses that will protect the eyes from ricocheting pellets or falling target pieces on the range. Many shooters understand that they have to wear glasses on a range, but they wouldn't consider wearing them in a hunting situation. It might surprise you to know that there are more dangers from things like in hunting situations that might cause eye damage than there are at an organized range. Stray pellets, tree branches and burning powder residue are three of the things that can cause eye damage in the field.

The safety value of eye protection is a given, but a good pair of shooting glasses can do much more than protect the eyes. The color of the lens is actually supposed to create a contrast between your target and the shooting background. There was a time that you could only buy shooting glasses with high visibility yellow or dark gray lenses. Well, those days have passed, and today you can find shooting glasses and interchangeable lens in a wide variety of colors.

A good rule of thumb when choosing a lens color is to use the lightest color possible without squinting. The high visibility yellow glasses that are common in many sporting goods stores are really made for indoor shooting. A pale yellow lens would work better for outside shooting. On extremely bright days, a dark brown lens seems to make the eyes comfortable. A good all around lens would be amber or vermilion in color.

Keep in mind that a dark lens color actually reduces light transmission to the eyes, much like dimming headlights at night in your car or truck. When your eyes get less light transmission, they also get less information from the target. So go with the lightest lens color you're comfortable with that will provide a contrast between the birds you are hunting and the shooting background.

Shooting glasses are an important part of a hunter's equipment. Not only do they provide protection for the eyes, when using the right color for contrast they can improve the shooter's ability to see their target more clearly.

CHAPTER

9

Shooting Styles and How They Apply

Let's review where we are. We've got the gun fitted. We know how to hold and mount the gun, and we know how to use our eyes to see leads and our hands to put the gun in place to take the shot. So now it's time to take the shot. The challenge for most wingshooters is how to deal with all of the speeds, angles and distances of the various game birds available to hunt.

If you're looking for a difference of opinion, just ask a wingshooter how much lead he sees when shooting a bird. Depending on the species of bird and type of hunting in question, you can count on a wide variety of answers that range from seeing no lead to what looks like the length of a school bus in front of a speeding target. What tends to be confusing here is that in many instances the shooters involved in a conversation on lead pictures have success at hitting their targets, but they all claim to see a different sight picture to do so.

With equal success in the face of different sight pictures, who's right? Well, the answer is that all of them are. After all, when used properly, they are hitting their share of birds, aren't they? Let's face it, the human race is filled with contrasting views of how each person sees the world. We see colors differently and our perception of distance,

speed and angles is certainly different. These differences explain why one shooter claims to shoot six feet ahead of a bird to hit it, while another says he sees very little forward allowance. Yet both of them have great success in the field.

For generations wingshooters around the world have developed shooting styles or methods that would increase their consistency in the field. Each of these styles was developed with specific target presentations in mind, as our shooting forefathers discovered what worked best for various game bird presentations through trial and error. Some styles tend to work better on flushing birds, while others are the ticket for long crossing shots. These methods were developed for the type of shots they encountered in a given shooting situation. But since there are so many different shot scenarios in the field, a one style fits all approach just doesn't work in wingshooting. The complete wingshooter understands this, so he has a mastery of different styles that can be used as shot presentations change.

It has already been determined that in order to hit a bird on the wing moving at an angle other than straight away, there has to be some form of forward allowance with the muzzle of the gun.

There are, of course, many variables that allow this to happen from shot to shot and shooter to shooter. The fact that shooters possess different visual and reflexive skills means that their physical reaction to mounting and swinging the gun, and their perception of a lead picture, is going to be different from person to person.

Since the muzzle of the gun has to be placed ahead of a bird in order to hit it, there has to be some reason that shooters can consistently hit similar shots using completely different lead pictures. The answer lies in the speed of the gun swing and the location of the muzzle relative to the bird as the stock comes to the face. Over the years, the differences in the physical and visual aspects of shooting have been developed into definitive shooting styles. So let's analyze the different recognized shooting styles to see how and why they work, as well as when a particular style might be better suited for a particular shot.

It should be noted here that you can only move the gun so far before the body starts to tighten up and slow the gun. Most shooters can move the muzzle comfortably, about six feet, relative to the insertion point. In other words, if you insert the gun directly on the bird, you can move to about six feet of lead without elevating your stress level.

Eye protection is critical in the field. You can't possibly know where shots are coming from, even if they are all taken above the horizon. It only takes one pellet. The key is to wear protective lenses that are made for shooting. Make sure they are high enough on the forehead for your eyes to focus down the rib through the lens.

This is why a precise insertion point for the style you choose to shoot is so important.

The top shooters have the ability to shoot all of the shooting styles. It is this knack of quickly identifying the bird, its speed, angle and distance that allows the accomplished wing shot to precisely place the muzzle of the gun in the right place in order to execute his chosen shooting style for that particular bird. And when the next target presents itself that shooter can again make split second decisions, which could mean that a totally different style would be better suited in order to make a successful shot.

The major variable in the wingshooting equation is the angle of presentation. The speed of the bird certainly plays a part, but it's the angle that dictates the perceived lead picture. Notice I said perceived lead. Let's assume that the distance to every bird shot during a day in the field is 30 yards from the gun and traveling at 40 miles per hour. The big difference in the shooter's lead picture would be determined by the angle of the shot. The more the target moves to a 90 degree crossing shot, the greater the lead, even though the bird would be the same distance from the gun when taken.

Shooters should keep in mind that the angles involved in hunting the various types of gamebirds tend to dictate the shooting style that would work comfortably. For instance, a bird flying in the direction of a shooter doesn't appear to be moving very fast at a distance, but the closer the bird gets to the gun, the faster it seems to be moving. For this reason, the shooter must make sure that the gun is moving at least at the pace of the bird once he initiates his move to the bird, his mount, swing and follow through. All of the shooting styles demand this technical movement for the shooter to be consistent. To get the gun moving towards the bird, shooters should try to catch the bird in the air with the forearm hand as they focus on it and mount the gun. This move will do more to get the gun into position than any other thing the shooter can do.

Such a move is most easily accomplished by focusing on the bird first and then moving the muzzle into position to execute the desired lead picture. When an intense target focus takes place and the shooter starts moving with it, he can effectively slow the target down. And when no target looks fast, inserting the gun in the desired spot to execute a chosen style is not difficult.

Most shooters have the skills to shoot only one way, so when the bird at hand doesn't present a comfortable flight path and distance for that style, the resulting shot usually produces a miss. And while some will argue that one style can be used for all shots, the vast majority of shooters cannot take the time to so precisely perfect a single style that will insure success on all the bird presentations encountered in the field. As a result, an understanding of the different styles and their particular advantages and disadvantages will be critical to improving your field shooting skills.

Regardless of which shooting style a shooter might employ, he will not be comfortable moving the gun a long distance once it is mounted. The foot and body position as the shot sequence commences will dictate the comfort zone or sweet spot where the shooter is most comfortable taking the shot.

As the gun comes to the face, the muzzle will be placed somewhere in the vicinity of the bird. That spot could be slightly behind the bird, on it or ahead of it. This muzzle position is referred to as the insertion point, and it is an important aspect of every shot and style. As the various shooting styles are discussed, the insertion point of the muzzle is often what will dictate which style is being used. And if the insertion point is wrong for the shooter's intended style, the result of the shot will likely be a miss.

THE SWING THROUGH METHOD

Without question, a sizeable percentage of wingshooters worldwide use the swing through, pull through or pass through method in the field. When using this method, the gun is mounted to the face behind the bird and then accelerated through its flight line. As the gun passes the target the trigger is squeezed, and hopefully the bird is harvested for the bag. Many shooters refer to this style as instinctive shooting, since the gun is simply pointed right at the target and the trigger is pulled as the gun goes past the bird.

There have been a number of highly recognized styles that use the basics of the swing through method for success. These styles were tried and proven in England many decades ago, where modern wingshooting as we know it was developed. Robert Churchill developed and promoted a style where the gun would come in to the target, usually from behind with the trigger being pulled the moment the gun touched the cheek. The shooter would see no lead picture whatsoever and have no conscious view of the barrel using Churchill's method, as the focus is totally on the target. Any forward allowance needed would be taken care of with gun speed, and the entire style is based on the shooter's ability to point. The most important aspect of the method was to match the flight line of the target and let the eyes and hands do the rest.

Churchill was a stocky gentleman who shot a rather short barreled side by side shotgun. Most of his shooting was on driven birds. When formulating this style, Churchill felt that the eyes and hands would find the right lead as the gun moved to and through the target. Since he was a stocky gentleman, his foot and body setup was more square to the target than other styles of the day.

The famous Holland and Holland Shooting School used much of Churchill's style, but took things a bit further by saying that the shooter should shoulder the gun and swing through the line of the bird before squeezing the trigger. The shooter's focus is on the bird, but there is an awareness of the muzzle of the gun. Additionally, the Holland and Holland style does not require that every shot be taken when the muzzle is right at the bird as it passes through. The style correctly identifies that all shooters are not alike, and recognizes that some will actually see some forward allowance on certain shots.

Shooting Styles and How They Apply | **119**

(far left) Robert Churchill perfected the Churchill style of shooting. The shooter stands square to the target in this style with the feet fairly close together. The shooter's weight shifts from one leg to another as the shooter moves through the swing radius. The opposite heel is always raised in this style.

(left) Percy Stanbury was also a great shooter. Stanbury's style called for the shooter's weight to always be on the front foot. The feet were positioned at one o'clock and three o'clock in the direction of the shot (for RH shooters). Moving the gun to a lead was acceptable in this style.

In America, the Orvis Shooting School style is very close to the Churchill and Holland and Holland methods. Students attending the school are taught to focus on the bird, bring the gun to its line, swing through the line and shoot the bird without any consciousness of a lead picture. Much of what the school teaches is very effective on flushing and close driven birds.

Needless to say, each of these styles when applied properly will mean success for a shooter, and all are dependent on the eyes and hands working as a team. Keep in mind, however, that the eyes focus first to give the hands and gun direction. Once they are understood and practiced consistently, they can be used on almost any shot one might encounter in the field.

In the purest form of the swing through method, the shooter will shoot directly at the bird as the gun passes through it. Because a lead is required on shots with any angle to them, the speed of the gun swing will be critical to the success of this method. And since the shooter actually sees no perceived lead with this style, the hands are proven to be quicker than the eye.

What makes the swing through style work without a defined lead picture is a little known phenomenon called "shooter's time." This is the time difference from when the eyes see that the gun is at the target to the time the trigger can actually be pulled. Since it takes about three tenths of a second or so for the eyes to send information to the brain to initiate a trigger pull, the gun has moved ahead of the bird even though the shooter's mind registered that he shot directly at the target. This is why gun speed and the timing of the trigger pull is so critical with this style.

The swing through method is particularly effective on flushing game such as quail, grouse, pheasants, etc. It is the generally accepted method on these types of birds because the hunter doesn't generally know exactly where the bird is, and he certainly has no guarantee of which direction or at what elevation it is likely to fly. Because of these reasons, the gun is invariably behind the bird as it flushes, so swinging through the bird is as natural an act as pointing your finger at it.

With this style, the shooter needs to quickly identify the speed of the bird with his eyes, since for the method to work the gun must be traveling faster than the bird. And to shoot the style in its orthodox form, the distance and angle of the shot will determine the speed of the swing to allow the shooter to always shoot at the target as he swings through it.

Since this style is based on the timing of the swing and trigger pull, it is critical that shooters who employ the swing through method find some consistency in where the gun is inserted behind the target so that it can move comfortably through the bird. If the shooter inserts the gun too far behind the bird, he will have problems getting to it, much less through and ahead of it as he continues to move the muzzle. In most cases the shooter will miss behind.

If the muzzle comes to the face and is too close to the target, chances are the shooter will miss in front as he accelerates the muzzle through the target. So you can see that finding a consistent insertion point just behind to the bird is a key element to the success of this method. Keep in mind that any deviation from this point will change the pace of the gun as it is moving through the target if the trigger is to be pulled at the bird. The farther behind a bird you mount and insert the gun, the faster you will have to swing to catch the bird. And rest assured that if you're playing chase to catch up with a bird to get to a lead picture, you will find inconsistencies in your game.

Another problem that many shooters encounter

with this style is that they push the gun to a spot behind the bird and then begin to swing the gun, instead of moving as the bird moves, and then inserting into its motion. As discussed earlier, the gun mount is a part of the swing. They are not two separate moves. As the eyes lock on the bird, the hands can move the gun into position behind the

target. Once it is moving, the gun can more easily swing through the bird.

Using this style, a right hand shooter will have a tendency to miss in front of a right to left bird and behind one moving left to right. The opposite is true for the left hand shooter. The differences in the sight picture seen between birds moving left or right can cause the eyes to play tricks on the shooter, so sticking with the orthodox style is important for success.

The gun is noticeably behind the bird in this shot. It might be tough to get the gun far enough ahead of this bird to hit it.

THE SWING THROUGH METHOD

Swing Through, Pass Through, Pull Through (all are one and the same). The swing through mehod of shooting is very popular with hunters and those who are self-taught and shoot instinctively. REMEMBER – successful, instinctive shooting comes as a RESULT of good technique. With swing through, the gun is always inserted behind the target. The bird is allowed to pass the line of the muzzle before any move is made. Control of speed of swing and timing are generally far more important to the swing through shooter than any lead picture. Some swing through shooters with good timing and a fast swing see little or no lead on most targets. The trigger is pulled on, or very near the bird as the mounted gun swings past the target.

This style can be very effective on driven birds that are taken in the 25 to 30 yard range. The old shooting adage, "butt, belly, beak, bang" really works well on these types of shots because of the speed of the muzzle. This hand speed usually gives the shooter the lead needed to take the bird cleanly because the shooter's eyes and brain can easily decipher when the forward allowance picture looks right.

The swing through style has been around for many years, and millions of birds have been harvested with it. Unfortunately, this style does have its limitations. Perhaps it is better said that the shooter has his limitations when applying this style to a speeding bird. The fact that most shooters really don't get enough practice generally spells trouble when the timing of the gun speed and trigger pull are so critical.

Let's not forget that timing is everything when applying a swing through style, so the pace of the muzzle and its insertion point are real keys to the success of this popular shooting style.

THE PULL AWAY METHOD

We have determined that shooting a shotgun, whether at birds or clay targets, is much akin to pointing your finger. This is because our natural ability allows us to visualize an object and instinctively point right at it. If the object is stationary, we have no problem putting a finger right on it. On the other hand, if it is in motion we still have the ability to point at it and follow its line. This is called eye/hand coordination, where the eyes lead the hands in a physical act. Since we have this inherent gift, it seems appropriate that we use it.

Because of this eye/hand coordination, the speed of the object we are pointing at is irrelevant. Somehow we can naturally decipher the speed, so regardless of how fast something is moving, we can get our hands to it and maintain its pace. Because the ability to point is so instinctive, it can be a real advantage in wingshooting, considering the complexities of how game birds can present themselves in the field.

A common occurrence in the field finds the shooter being surprised by a bird. This surprise triggers our instinct to point, and quite often the result of pointing at the target while keeping the gun moving with it is another bird in the bag. If the gun comes to the face behind the bird and sweeps through the flight line, a successful shot is made using the swing through method. If the gun follows a line to intercept the bird in flight and the muzzle moves away from it to a lead picture before the trigger is squeezed, this is more along the lines of the pull away method.

The pull away style offers the distinct advantage of initially allowing the shooter to keep the target in focus and in contact with the gun, since with this style the gun and target are always in view together as the muzzle moves to the insertion point and then to the face and shoulder. Once the gun is mounted, the shooter is not only focused on the bird, he has also matched its speed with the muzzle. By using the bird as a point of reference and quickly computing its pace, the shooter will almost never find himself rushed. When a shooter can match his pace with his target's pace, he doesn't have to chase the bird across the field. And not playing chase allows the gun to be positioned for the shot more quickly and with more control.

Getting a feel for how much lead a shooter should see on a particular shot will be an individual challenge. The speed of the gun moving away from the bird will dictate the distance. A quick pull away means less perceived lead, because the shooter's time discussed earlier effects pull away too. A slower and smoother pull away means that a bit more visible lead might be needed. In most instances, the speed of the bird and its angle flight will determine how the gun is pulled away for the shot. Realistically the shooter should not concern himself with precise lead pictures. With this style the most important thing to remember is that the gun is pulled away from the insertion point. As the lead picture develops and feels right, the trigger is pulled as the gun continues to move for the follow through.

Experience will ultimately help you determine how much lead you need to see. Never forget that the more a bird crosses in front of the gun, the more lead it will take to hit it. And keep in mind that if you shoot where a bird was, it will never

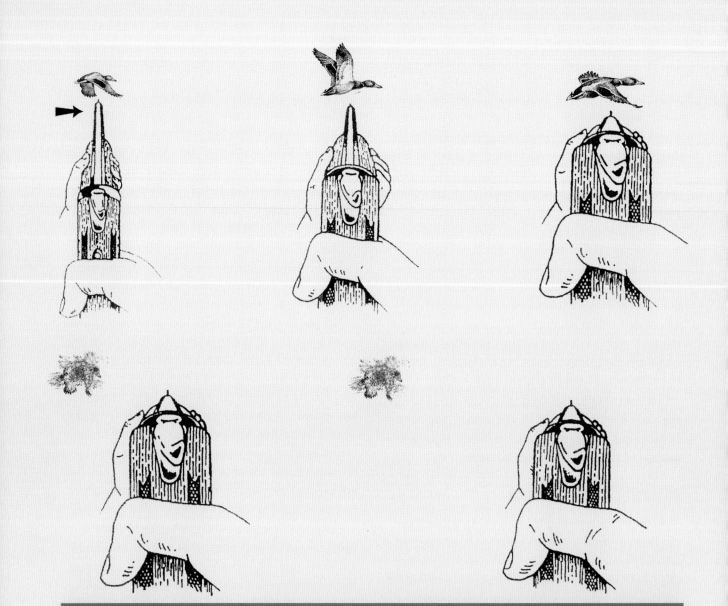

THE PULL AWAY METHOD

This is the official CPSA shooting method. With pull away, the gun is mounted directly at the target. This method uses our natural ability to point. Pull away enables a shooter to judge speed, distance and line of the target very effectively. Stance, timing and rhythm of the shot, as with all shooting techniques, are determined by the pre-planned kill zone. After the stock touches the face, the gun is smoothly moved ahead of the target until the correct lead picture is seen and felt. Pull away is excellent for long range shots and can improve shooter timing and consistency on many shots.

wind up in your bag in your bag. Don't be afraid to see lead, and your instincts will tell you when to pull the trigger.

As you can see, the differences between pull away and swing through are subtle, with the major difference being the insertion point of the muzzle when the stock comes to the face. If the gun comes into the line of the bird and on it, the style is pull away. Some shooters start slightly behind the bird and come through it to acquire the line. Since the gun continues to move forward until the right lead is seen, this is still considered a form of pull away. On particularly long crossing birds, they might insert the gun slightly ahead of the target before pulling away. So as you can see, making adjustments to lead pictures can be pretty simple.

So when would a shooter want to employ the pull away style in the field? Swing through shooters typically have trouble with crossing targets because they cannot moderate the speed of the muzzle to accommodate target distance and speed as the angles and distances change. Keep in mind that, with that style, the gun is always moving faster than the bird, and the farther away a bird of a crossing nature is, more forward allowance is required to hit it. Let's face it. The farther and/or faster a bird is from the gun, the more stress it puts on the shooter. The pull away method helps ease that stress on tough birds in the field because the bird is always the focal point of the method.

When using the pull away style, reading the speed of the bird is important, but since the gun moves to intercept the target and match its speed at the insertion point, it is easier to get the muzzle ahead of the bird. If you want to explain this method in simple terms, try move, mount, picture and shoot. Taking the time to identify that the picture is right is important, and it only takes mere tenths of a second.

So for shooters who find themselves under stress to get the muzzle of the gun to the target and ahead of it, the pull away style might be a salvation. And since the style uses our pointing ability, it is by far the most forgiving of all shooting methods.

THE MAINTAINED LEAD METHOD

Some shooters have a better understanding than others about how to see a lead picture. They realize early on that in order to hit a moving target with some defined angle to its flight path requires some forward allowance of the muzzle. Most skeet shooters, for instance, claim to shoot a style known as maintained lead. With this style, the muzzle of the gun comes to the shooter's face at a predetermined lead ahead of the target and stays at that lead picture until the trigger is pulled and a follow through occurs.

In the field, the maintained lead method is most successful on birds that present themselves at angles requiring definitive lead pictures such as crossers, overhead shots and birds with extreme speed and complex angles. The reason for this, of course, is because the only way to hit such birds is to get the muzzle of the gun in front of them.

Shooters who shoot with lead pictures will find that they will have more success if they avoid starting the muzzle of the gun too far behind the bird. To get to their desired picture, such an insertion point would cause them to swing through the bird and then try to find their lead. It is important that the gun not be on the shoulder for an extended period of time, and such a move could disrupt the shooter's timing. Sometimes "riding" the bird or looking at it too long down the muzzle can cause the shooter to divert his eyes from the bird and back to the gun to make sure the picture is what he thinks is right.

At the same time, the unpredictable nature of the flight line a bird might take is reason enough to get the right sight picture as quickly as possible and get the trigger squeezed. Remember that the longer the gun is in the shoulder, the more chance the shooter has to make a mistake, so finding the lead picture by getting the gun in position quickly is one advantage of maintained lead.

Finding the right lead picture in the field is no different from shooting the maintained lead style on clay targets. It works best when the shooter looks at the leading edge or front of the target on birds that are not too fast or at a great distance. If the bird is moving at a rapid pace or is at a distance of 30 or more yards, the shooter can visually pick up the bird, but actually focus ahead of it so that the muzzle of the gun will travel to that point. The experts will tell you not to worry so much about a specific lead picture, since the eyes will naturally help you determine when the lead is just right. In most cases, however, if you are missing a long crossing bird, chances are you need more lead than you're giving it. On long crossing shots or extremely fast birds, chances are pretty good that by starting the muzzle behind the target, you won't be able to get to the desired lead before the body runs out of swing and the trigger has to be pulled. It's a terrible feeling to know you are going to miss a bird, but you find yourself pulling the trigger anyway.

Remember it's sometimes best to shoot to miss, and maintained lead is the perfect style to make that happen. When using the maintained lead style, the gun is inserted ahead of a bird, it moves at the bird's pace as the lead picture is found. When the shooter recognizes his insertion as the right picture, he simply moves with the bird and pulls the trigger. It should be noted that keeping the gun moving after the shot is important because the gun and target are traveling at the same speed with this style, and any deviation of the gun speed will affect the lead picture. The more the bird crosses in front of the gun, the better this method will work.

Unfortunately many shooters try to force the maintained lead style on birds that are better shot with either pull away or swing through. This is especially true on targets that are presented with a quartering away angle or less like flushing quail, pheasant or grouse. Shooters would be wise to note that the farther a quartering bird flies, the less lead it requires since the bird's angle diminishes as it flies away from the shooter. So if they get the gun ahead of such a bird, and maintain a lead, they are unintentionally increasing the lead as the target flies. In these instances, the swing through or pull away methods might be more useful.

Most hunters can't tell you what shooting style they use. If the truth is known, the majority of them employ some hybrid of two styles. The key to successful shooting in the field is consistency. Remember that you don't want to chase birds to get to a lead, and you don't want to ride the target to double check the lead. You've got to have enough confidence to pull the trigger when the lead looks right.

DON'T FORGET THE PICTURE

Regardless of which shooting style you choose to employ, there are a few elements of each shot that must remain constant. As the bird is visually acquired, you will move the gun to the insertion

point, mount the gun, identify the picture and shoot the bird.

In many instances shooters tend to execute parts of this exercise, but they most often leave out the picture identification. Keep in mind that wingshooting is all about seeing lead pictures. As discussed earlier, the eyes will identify when the picture looks right, and you should trust them. In most cases they are right, and the moment they tell you so, you should take the shot. This entire shot sequence will take only seconds, but each element must be in place for you to have success.

MULTIPLE BIRDS/MULTIPLE SHOOTING STYLES

Once a shooter learns how to use the various shooting styles in the field, he can become a very accomplished shot, since he can react efficiently to virtually any bird presentation. As his proficiency increases, chances are he will have the opportunity to take two or even three or more birds from a flock or covey if the limits allow him to do so. In order to accomplish this consistently, it's necessary for a shooter to deal with the complexities

When hunting flushing birds, you my have to use multiple shooting styles as the birds move away from the gun.

found as changes in the speed, angle and distance of his targets occur.

First of all, game birds have to be shot one at a time. This simply means that a shooter must pick one target and stick with it visually until the shot is successful. Of course, when there are a number of birds in the air, this can be a problem for the inexperienced shooter, which points to why target focus is so very critical. Wingshooters are notori-

ous for flock shooting, a mistake which typically results in an emptied gun and no birds in the bag.

Being able to harvest multiple birds with a series of shots is a matter of good planning and shot management. If a shooter can pick which bird he shoots first so that additional targets can be attempted in the same shot series, his chances of doubles or triples are significantly increased. He must, however, be successful on the first bird

before he can claim the second, so his mechanics and technique need to be solid on the first shot.

There are two trains of thought to be considered when shooting multiple birds in an individual series of shots. Some shooters want to shoot what they think is the easiest bird they see first, and

Birds such as waterfowl, doves and pigeons provide a variety of speeds, angles and distances once the first shot is taken near a flock.

take their chances on any others that could be added to the bag during the shot sequence. Experienced shooters are able to visualize how multiple birds can be taken, and will generally leave the easier birds for the second and third shots.

Regardless of which birds a shooter takes first, the most important part of harvesting multiple targets is making sure that the focus remains on one bird at a time. Once that bird is down, the eyes can shift to a second one, and should remain focused on it until it is downed.

Sometimes the way birds present themselves to the shooter can demand the use of multiple shooting styles in a single series of shots. Let's say, for instance, that you are hunting doves over a grain field. It's a particularly good shoot, and many birds are flying. You see a small flock of birds coming towards you. Your first shot is overhead, and since the birds are fairly high, you elect to shoot take the first shot using maintained lead. As you get your lead, the trigger is pulled and there is success with the first shot, leaving time for a chance at a double. But now the birds are high and quartering away from you. Keeping in mind that as a quartering bird flies, the lead to harvest it lessens, you focus on a bird and sweep the gun through it. The swing through style brings success on the second bird, when trying to apply maintained lead to it would have likely been futile. As you can see, understanding how to apply various styles based on target presentation is key to your success.

In most instances the gun speed will increase once the eyes focus on a second bird. As a result of a quicker gun, it is common for the lead picture on the second or third bird of a sequence to be slightly less. Just remember that the eyes get to the target first and give the hands and gun direction.

Which shooting style or styles a shooter might use is usually a matter of personal preference or training. It has been discussed here that all of these styles can be successful when used properly. At the same time, certain styles tend to work better on certain types of shots. Shooters who are flexible enough to learn more than one shooting style and when to use them will find more consistency in their shooting game both on clays and in the field.

Mastering the Common Mistakes for Misses

Many wingshooters have a difficult time understanding why they miss birds. Realistically there aren't that many mistakes that a shooter can make when he attempts a shot, and in most instances one problem often creates another. Perhaps by identifying potential problems individually, you can see where the potential for misses lie and, as a result, take the practice steps necessary to alleviate such mistakes.

Of course, identifying the problem is only part of the equation. You must also fix the problem. Listed below are the seven most common reasons a hunter or shooter misses a flying target or bird. Sometimes shooters make more than one of these mistakes, but fixing the right one first can lead to minimizing other problems.

POOR TIMING

A major problem that many shooters seem to have when shooting afield is poor timing. This can be a result of virtually anything from having the gun out of position to get it on the shoulder properly, to an inconsistent gun pace relative to the pace of the target or an overzealous trigger hand racing to mount the gun.

Poor timing can be a reason for missing that might occur at any time, and can be most easily cured by proper target focus, a good gun mount and solid technique. The problems with a shooter's timing are most often caused by a lack of concentration and an inconsistent gun swing relative to the speed, angle and distance of his target. When a shooter fails to recognize and react to these target characteristics, chances are that a miss is imminent.

Timing is based on how a shooter moves relative to the movement of his target. Chances are if he overreacts to a flushing or passing bird, for instance, he will rush the gun past it before the trigger can be pulled. On the other hand, if he is slow to swing the gun when a bird presents itself, he will invariably wind up behind his target.

Let's not forget that the most accomplished wingshooters you will ever see look to be in slow motion. They only react to the speed of the bird they are attempting to harvest, and they can change their speed to compensate for the speed of the target. They do this by making sure that step one in the shot process is visual focus on a chosen target. When the birds are fast, they move fast. When they are slow, they move slow. Once

Once you get yourself properly positioned in advance of a shot, it's much easier to focus on the bird and move the gun to a precise insertion point.

a shooter's eyes have focused on a bird, the most important part of the shot sequence is to move as the bird moves, and then a bit more to execute a chosen shooting style and complete the shot.

By matching up his initial pace with that of the bird, the shooter will always be able to comfortably get his gun in position to make a clean kill, and he will find that keeping his target in view with the gun mounted will be much easier. This will be the case regardless of which shooting style is used, since the speed of the gun for pull away and swing through don't increase until the insertion point is made.

FOCUSING ON THE GUN AND NOT THE TARGET

One of the more common reasons that shooters miss in the field is because they focus more on the gun than on the target. In other words, they are in effect aiming at the bird. Most shooters got their shooting legs at an early age by plinking away with a .22 caliber rifle. Unfortunately the only similarity between rifles, shotguns and pistols is that they are all classified as firearms. Shooting them is as different as day and night.

In order to consistently hit a target using a precise aiming point with a rifle or pistol, the shooter must align front and rear sights with a focus primarily on the sights. In most cases the targets for rifle and pistol shooting are stationary, which allows the shooter the time to make his precise sight alignment. Herein lies the main difference between these three types of firearms.

In wingshooting the targets fly at various rates of speed, and a successful shot requires the shooter to focus on the target and not the gun. Since a shotgun has no visible rear sight, the shooter's master eye serves as the sight. As a result, the eye and the front bead on the shotgun have to align perfectly when the gun is mounted to the face and shoulder if the gun is to shoot where the eyes look.

In many instances, however, the shooter wants to make sure that this alignment is correct, and the tendency is to transfer the eyes from the target back to the gun. Once the eyes shift to the gun, the shooter loses touch with his target. When this happens, the shooter will attempt to find the bird again. Since the eyes lead the hands in shotgunning, the gun will go to the bird rather than to the proper lead, which in turn affects the timing of the shot.

The correct procedure for the shooter to be successful is to focus on the bird while having a soft focus on the muzzle of the gun. In other words, the shooter must be aware of the gun without aiming

Many rifle shooters struggle with focusing on the target, since they learned to shoot by focusing on the sights of the rifle. The learning curve to move these rifle shooters to shotgun shooters could be significant.

at the target, and by looking beyond the gun and to the target, the gun should shoot where he looks. Can you see now how important visual focus is to a successful shot? Having an idea of the type of lead picture required will certainly simplify this procedure, but as we have already established, it is amazing how the eyes find the proper lead picture when the shooter does everything else right.

POOR GUN MOUNT

Once a shooter has fitted his gun properly, a large number of his misses will be a result of a poor gun mount. As alluded to earlier, the mechanics of a proper gun mount are critical to

shooting success.

It's important to keep in mind that mastering the motor skills required to mount the gun consistently in the same spot on the face and shoulder every time does require practice. Unfortunately, the majority of casual bird hunters would never think of practicing gun mounts on a daily, or at least periodic basis, like many of the top clay shooters do.

The difference between that casual shooter and a seasoned sporting clays enthusiast is easily noted, but both of them have to be able to mechan-

The muzzle of the gun should be steered to the lead picture with minimal movement. This is best controlled by positioning the gun just under the armpit, with the muzzle elevation starting just under the line of the bird

When the gun is noticeably out of place relative to the target, the shooter rarely has time to recover quickly enough to make a successful shot.

ically mount the gun to be successful. Perhaps that's why most competitive sporting clays shooters often fare better on live birds than their trap or skeet counterparts. Being able to properly control the movement of the gun's muzzle starts with a mastery of the gun mount, and once the muscle movement for the mount has been memorized the shooter will find it easier to get the gun in position for a successful shot.

Don't forget that a proper gun mount is a push to the bird and insertion point and a lift of the stock to the face with the trigger hand. The hands work as a team, with neither exerting more push or lift than the other. And since gun mounts can be practiced away from the range and field, getting the proper mechanics dialed in perfectly is simply a matter of time and a desire to do so.

INCORRECT TECHNIQUE

When a shooter misses a bird because of incorrect technique, it is generally accepted that his mistakes were the result of trying to apply a certain shooting style that didn't comfortably suit the target he was shooting. We have established that any of the various recognized shooting styles used worldwide will work for a shooter as long as the technique is applied properly. The main reason that incorrect technique misses birds is because most shooters don't fully understand the orthodox use of recognized shooting styles.

A shooter should always keep in mind that the more a bird crosses in front of him, the more forward allowance or lead will be required to successfully hit it. As a result, if he is shooting at a bird that requires a good bit of lead, it would generally be a mistake to start the gun well behind the bird to obtain that lead.

At the same time, if a bird presents itself in a manner that doesn't take much forward allowance, he can't expect consistent success if the gun mounts too far ahead of the bird. If a shooter feels that he is well ahead of his target, chances are he'll have problems slowing the gun to get the right lead.

Regardless of which style he uses, his chances of a successful shot will improve if he remembers

to match his pace with that of the bird early in the shot sequence. This will help make a precise insertion point much easier.

STOPPING THE GUN

Certainly one of the major reasons a shooter misses could be traced to our rifle shooting heritage. Since most shooters learned to shoot by aiming a rifle or pistol, chances are they will occasionally find themselves unable to get the gun sufficiently through or ahead of the bird. When a shooter's smoothness of swing is interrupted this way, he will invariably stop the gun. If the muzzle ever stops, even briefly, the timing of the shot will be affected and the possibilities of a miss are increased.

A shooter can minimize stopping the gun by heightening his concentration and focusing on the bird, being smooth with the gun swing and remembering to follow through after the shot is taken. By concentrating on these aspects of a successful shot, the shooter can assure himself a good chance every time he shoulders the gun.

Two ways to make certain that the guy doesn't stop is to watch the bird fall through the beads of the gun or staying in the gun as if you were going to shoot at the bird again. While these two tips sound simple, if you can make them a part of every shot in the field your shooting success will increase significantly.

A great deal of the success or failure experienced by a shooter is determined by the confidence he has in seeing lead pictures. The more often a shooter sees a bird fall or a target break with a lead picture, the more confidence he will have the next time he sees a similar shot.

Since the rear sight on a shotgun is the shooter's eyes, and a proper gun fit allows the gun to shoot where the shooter is looking, it is important to bring the gun to your face and focus on the target through the beads on the gun.

JERKING THE TRIGGER

It's pretty rare for the average hunter to find himself jerking the trigger or flinching when shooting live birds. This phenomenon is typically found in the intense competitive clay target shooter, who has shot literally thousands and thousands of rounds of ammunition over the years.

A flinch is best described as a mental refusal of a physical act, such as pulling the trigger. In other words, even though the shooter attempts to pull the trigger, the brain sends a message to the muscles in the trigger finger that will not allow it to move. This is most often the result of a fear of missing or the anticipation of recoil, and is almost always followed by the trigger being jerked with little or no success.

When shooting birds, hunters will usually not refuse to pull the trigger, rather they have a tendency to yank the trigger and fire the gun before it is properly positioned on the shoulder. When this happens, of course, the timing of the shot is significantly affected and the target is usually not hit.

This typically occurs on flushing birds or when the shooter is surprised by the sudden appearance of a bird. Sometimes in a rush to get off a shot, the shooter gets into the trigger too quickly. The flinch in hunting can be eliminated if the shooter realizes that he usually has more time to execute a shot than he thinks. There are no gamebirds that can outrun a speeding shotstring, so rushing a shot just isn't necessary. By slowing down his approach to shooting the bird and giving his eyes time to focus on a specific target, the shooter will have better control of his movements and the technique required to properly mount and swing the gun. If the shooter will stay in the gun by keeping his head down and his eyes through the rib in order to watch the bird fall, he will be less concerned with shooting too quickly.

When more than one bird is presented in the kill zone, like here with this covey rise, you must choose your target one at a time. There's always more time than you think.

It's been said that 60 percent of shooting is confidence. That's confidence in yourself, confidence in the gun and confidence in your ammo. Having this level of certainty that a successful shot can be made by taking the time to properly position the gun will certainly improve one's percentages of success afield.

LIFTING THE HEAD OFF THE STOCK

Of all the reasons for missing birds, lifting the head off the stock is probably the the most common of all. Remember that a properly fitted shotgun will allow the eyes and the gun to look and shoot to the same spot. That's the beauty of pointing the gun rather than aiming it. So when you look through the beads on the rib of the gun, it will shoot where the eyes look. Don't look at the beads. Just be aware of them, much like you are aware of the white lines in the center of the road when driving. You are aware of them, but your focus never goes there.

This holds true time after time, and successful shots are made consistently unless the eye/barrel/bird relationship changes. But when the head is lifted off the stock or the eyes are lifted above the sighting plane of the gun, this constitutes a change in where the eyes and gun look, which will usually constitute a miss.

A fairly common occurrence with clay shooters is not lifting the head, but merely lifting the eyes above the rib to get a better look at the target. This is especially true on targets that are dropping or have a descending line of flight. The results, however, are generally the same, and they aren't good. Shooters guilty of lifting the eyes should remember to concentrate on their targets through the rib of the gun. Failure to do so will usually cause the gun to stop.

There are a number of reasons for the head to lift as the trigger is being pulled. If the drop on the stock is too low for the shooter, the eyes will be below the receiver and the face will have to be lifted in order to correctly see the bird beyond the muzzle. Proper gun fit, of course, will cure the problem if this is the case.

If the gun is mounted improperly, it will be

Once the head comes off the gun, the rear (eyes) and front (bead) sights on the gun are no longer aligned. This will most certainly cause a miss. Since the shot has been taken, was the cheek pressure released early or after the shot?

With the gun properly mounted your head should be fairly erect, with the eyes focused through the gun and to the target.

difficult for the shooter to get his sight picture adjusted in the short time that a shooter generally has to take a shot at a speeding bird. Since the eyes should attempt to follow the bird, they will want to stay focused on it, so they could leave the stock if it isn't positioned in the cheek and on the shoulder properly. Consistent gun mount practice will add to the timeliness of a proper picture and shot.

The angle of ascent or descent of a bird in flight will also cause the shooter to lift his head off the gun. If a bird flushes and rises quickly, the shooter's tendency is to first lift the eyes above the gun to find the bird. If the eyes stay up as the bird rises, there's a good chance that the head will come up as well. If the bird is dropping or landing, if the shooter allows it to come to the gun, chances are he will lift his head in order to keep it in sight just on top of the rib.

It has been established that in shotgun shooting the eyes lead the hands to the target and subsequently to the correct lead picture. And as long as the gun mount is correct, the head can stay down as the muzzle moves along the target line. If the lead picture is right, a successful shot will be the result.

So there you have it, a series of examples of why you miss. By identifying these individual problems and providing a fix for them, there is a good possibility that your skills in the field will improve significantly.

Doves
and Such

Major ammunition manufacturers often report that there are more shotgun shells fired on the opening day of dove season in America than any other day of the year. Whether that statistic is right or not is questionable, but one thing is certain. The dove is the most shot at and missed of all game bird species. Each year, to the delight of ammo makers, tens of millions of rounds of ammunition are fired at these little gray bullets.

There are a number of different species of doves that hunters actively pursue each year. The most common of these species in North America is the mourning dove, with the whitewing dove running a distant second. In most of South America the eared dove is the primary species hunted. This dove species tends to be slightly smaller than the mourning dove, but it is available in simply staggering numbers. The speedy, high flying African turtle dove often hunted in Morocco is one of the world's most difficult wingshooting targets. There are other dove species than those mentioned, but rest assured that all of them offer a significant challenge.

In many parts of the world, wingshooters pursue a number of pigeon species. Pigeons come in a variety of sizes, from the large and tough to bring down wood pigeon in England to the spot wing and picazuro pigeons of South America and the acrobatic rock pigeon found in the rocky cliffs of South Africa. Pigeon shooting in America is pretty much limited to the feral pigeon found around farmsteads and feed lots. If you've ever shot any of the pigeon species, you know that they are a tough bird to harvest.

Dove and pigeons are from the same family and have similar habits. These bird species tend to feed early in the morning and again in the afternoon. At some point they will seek water before going to roost. As with virtually all wildlife species, their numbers tend to vary depending on the supply of water and food. Both species prefer more open ground for feeding, but if necessary they will land on seed pods of plants like sunflowers to pick seeds right off the pods.

The mourning dove and whitewing dove in North America are both migratory species. They tend to be quite susceptible to changes in temperature, and in many instances they are headed South with the first cool snap of Fall. There are many stories out there about fields full of birds the day before a hunt, but none on hunt day. As a result, the seasoned dove hunter knows that when the birds are in his hunting location, he's got to get them while he can.

READING YOUR HUNTING LOCATION

The hunter can read a feeding field or water source in order to determine the best spot to set up for a daily hunt. Since these birds are creatures of habit, they will tend to fly the same pattern into and out of the field day after day.

When entering a field, hunters should look for objects that tend to attract dove or pigeons. Things like power lines through the field, tall pine trees, a pond or water source adjacent to the field

One of the most popular forms of wingshooting is dove hunting. Seasons start in the U.S. in September, which signals the start of the hunting season.

One of the most sporting targets anywhere in the world is the spot-winged pigeon. This bird was taken in Argentina.

These birds were also shot in Argentina in just over two hours one afternoon.

or a large tree with bare limbs tend to attract birds as they sometimes land in them before entering a field.

Once the birds do start to come in, they will usually do so regardless of the shooting pressure. Their sole purpose is to find either food or water before returning to the trees to rest during the day or roost in the evening. If none of the aforementioned objects are available, look for a high spot in the field or an area where the tree cover is low. These birds would rather come in fairly low so they can get to the food or water source quickly.

BE PREPARED FOR ANYTHING

A hot dove or pigeon shoot will offer the hunter a variety of shot presentations. And because these birds tend to have excellent vision, it is important for hunters to conceal themselves or keep a low profile in their setup if cover is not available.

Hunters should wear either camouflage or neutral colors that best match their hunting surroundings. But the most important thing a hunter can do is remain still as birds approach, since any movement will be detected. It's a good bet that hunter movement is responsible for the birds taking evasive action more than any other reason.

Many hunters choose to sit on stools or low profile chairs in when shooting these species.

If a shot is to be taken from a seated position, the hunter must first position himself prior to mounting the gun to insure a comfortable transition of the gun through the kill zone. Failure to shift the body to allow the hands to move the gun through the target kill zone will often result in the shooter running out of swing and a missed shot.

**Doves often go to water before they go to roost.
They prefer shorelines with little or no vegetation.
Decoys can help bring them into range.**

(right) Since a vertical shot greatly extends the body, slipping your forearm hand down an inch or two will give you more extension to finish the shot and follow through.

If the birds are coming fairly high and straight overhead, the first shot should be taken between 50 and 60 degrees in order for follow up shots to be effective. On shots straight above the shooter's head, the front or forearm hand can be moved a half inch or so closer to the receiver to give the shooter more extension for the shot.

If the birds are coming in low enough where the first shot can be taken at a 45 degree angle, you should have the confidence to take the shot. Doing so will buy you time for a follow up shot if you need one or if you wish to take another bird. Other angles in front or to the side of the shooter usually require a slight position change in the body while seated to allow enough lateral movement in the gun swing.

This approach will work while shooting from a standing position as well. Make sure, however, that you position your feet slightly closer together in order to have the vertical swing radius to finish the shot sequence.

PICK YOUR TARGET – ONE AT A TIME

Since doves and pigeons tend to fly in flocks, it is important to pick out one bird as a target. Once that selected bird is dropped, the eyes can shift to

another one. The hard focus on a single target is absolutely critical, because these birds also move horizontally with each wing beat. As a result, they crisscross in flight. This intense focus will help the shooter keep his head down on the stock as he follows through with the shot. You can bet that if the shooter sees other birds in the flock once the gun is mounted, he will most like lift his face off the gun, which will tend to stop the muzzle. A shooter can break the entire shot sequence down to this

Pick one bird and stick with it before moving to another one.

very simple point. As long as the target is moving, the muzzle of the gun has to be moving too if you want success.

A common mistake that shooters make in a dove field is mounting the gun well before they plan to take the shot. As discussed in an earlier chapter, the gun should not be mounted until the shooter plans to execute the shot. If a hunter makes this mistake, he will likely find that the birds race past the gun muzzle, forcing him to chase the target from behind. Keep in mind that once the gun is mounted, the shooter has signaled that he intends to take the shot. If the target is not yet in range, the gun shouldn't be put into play.

WHY SO LITTLE SUCCESS?

According to most experts, doves are the most difficult to hit of the game bird species we hunt, with the average being around one bird for every five shells expended. There are a number of reasons for this, but the primary reason is that doves are small birds that can fly about 45 miles per hour on a calm day, and much faster with a tail wind.

When doves are passing by hunters, their line of flight tends to vary from side to side, but once they spot the movement of a hunter they are capable of making quick twists and turns that simply defy the laws of flight. This sudden flight path change is usually temporary, so hunters can often hold off for a moment and then take the shot at the birds going away.

Many hunters try to shoot doves or pigeons with the same shooting style and approach as they would flushing or decoying birds. This tends to be a mistake since the speed of the birds and the more pronounced shot angles encountered when shooting them is totally different from most other game bird species. There are simply more crossing targets when shooting doves and pigeons than in any other type of wingshooting.

As discussed earlier, the more a target presents itself in a crossing fashion, the more lead it will take to hit that target, and seeing a lead picture on shot angles approaching a perpendicular angle to the shooter is critical for consistent success. When shooting doves or pigeons, more birds have to be missed in front if the hunter is going to hit his target. In other words, they take more lead than most hunters think.

You'll find that the very best shots on doves and pigeons fully understand how to change shooting styles to match the angles, speeds and distances presented by these fast flying birds. They know how to read the birds in flight and they never let the bird fly too far past the muzzle of the gun. In the vast majority of cases matching target speed with the muzzle and body will insure a comfortable transition to the proper sight picture. The best shooters can exhibit this ability shot after shot.

The very best of dove shots never look like they are in a hurry. They understand that they have to exercise complete control over the muzzle, and that the gun only needs to move slightly more than does the target. All of the shooting styles can be applied to doves and pigeons, but shooters who

employ either pull away, maintained lead or a combination of the two tend to have more success on the crossing shots.

USE THE RIGHT EQUIPMENT

If there is one game bird that stirs emotion amongst hunters regarding gun and ammo selection, it has to be the dove. Pigeon hunters know to bring the "lumber" so to speak, but dove hunting enthusiasts tend to shoot everything from a beefy 12 gauge packed with heavy field loads to

the diminutive .410 loaded with half ounce loads of hope.

There is a distinct difference between doves harvested early in the season and those taken weeks or months later. Hunts early in the season often encounter a sizable number of young birds. As the season progresses and the birds get larger and stronger, they also get tougher to harvest.

It's not uncommon for small gauge guns and low velocity loads of number eight or nine shot to do the job early in the season. The birds get bigger and tougher as the season progresses, so many hunters go the either 12 or 20 gauge guns loaded with an ounce or more of seven and a half shot. What gun and load a hunter chooses is certainly personal, but the old saying, "use enough gun" even applies to doves at some point in the season.

Using chokes between improved cylinder and modified will usually give a hunter his best chance of success. Doves aren't difficult to kill, but like any game bird, the right amount of shot and pellet energy has to be placed in the right spot to do the job quickly.

So if you want to improve your average come opening day, work on your target focus, gun mounts and insertion points on a clays range in the off season, and use good common sense when choosing your equipment. Dove hunting tends to be a very social outdoor endeavor, and when you shoot well on the day, you tend to be a bit more sociable.

Your goal should be more birds with fewer shells. Of course when you go to exotic places with liberal or no limits, you can shoot a lot of shells in a short time.

The Wonders of Waterfowling

For generations, wingshooters have held the various waterfowl species found in their region in high reverence. There's just something about duck and goose hunting that stirs something within us. Perhaps it's the beauty of a breathtaking sunrise or the anxious twitch of a well-trained retriever. Whatever the reason, the tradition of waterfowl hunting has stood the test of time, and items like decoys and calls are often looked upon as highly collectable heirlooms.

Many waterfowl hunters have problems harvesting ducks and geese with any consistency because of a number of reasons. Things like reading speed and distance, learning to shoot non-toxic shot, shooting from awkward positions and identifying targets all tend to complicate matters. But a successful day hunting waterfowl doesn't have to be any different from any other day afield. Let's look at how you can increase your success in the duck blind and the goose pit.

First of all, to have a successful waterfowl day, you've got to be where ducks and/or geese want to be. Setting up in the parking lot of your local sporting goods store usually won't provide you with much action, but good scouting to find the right hunting location can pay huge dividends. And being at that right place at the right time can mean the difference between just another cold day in the marsh and a great day in the blind.

Since waterfowl have tremendous vision, proper

concealment is a critical element to a great day in the duck marsh. Matching colors in order to blend in to the background is crucial, and the use of camouflage netting, prefab blind material and/or natural vegetation can be the difference between success and failure.

With the exception of the wild turkey, waterfowl may have the best vision of all game birds. They have an uncanny ability to pick up the slightest movement, and anything that looks unnatural to them as they fly over your hunting location can send them off looking for another landing spot. Many hunters make the mistake of exposing their hands and face to birds at just the wrong time, so if you must look up or move your arms, it's important to do it at the right time. If you must move, do so when the birds are to your side or going away from you.

If hunters had the chance to see what the birds see from overhead, they would wonder why any self respecting duck or goose would ever come in to a decoy spread. In many instances they can see movement, shiny faces, reflections off of gun barrels and spent hulls, and much more. Make sure that you look at your blind from above if possible, because that's what the birds will see. Except for some sea ducks, their view is not from ground or water level. Pick up anything that looks out of place, and you'll have a chance at more shot opportunities.

A good decoy rig can be very helpful if placed in the right spot. In other words, there's more to putting out decoys than simply throwing them out randomly. Today's commercially produced decoys are much lighter in weight than their hand carved counterparts of yesteryear. As a result, larger spreads are possible.

Puddle duck spreads are usually placed differently than are diver or sea duck rigs. Puddle ducks consist of those species that lift off the water vertically. They are commonly hunted from coast to coast in North America, with the most common puddler being the mallard. Other puddle duck species include pintail, widgeon, gadwall, teal, wood duck and shoveler.

Since they feed by picking vegetation or insects

Ducks have tremendous vision. They can pick up the slightest movement, causing them to flare. A good blind and camo help even the odds.

(left) There's more to hunting than shooting. Putting out decoys is an important part of any duck hunt.

(right) Green timber duck hunting is truly waterfowling in its purest form. No blind is required, as hunters can stand next to or behind trees that have been flooded by man or Mother Nature.

off the water or by tipping their bodies upward to feed on vegetation under water, they usually prefer more shallow water for feeding. They are particularly fond of grain crops such as rice, corn, milo and soy beans. In wooded or marshy areas their food sources include seeds, insects and acorns.

Most shots at puddle ducks will be taken as the birds are decoying and then moving back up vertically. If a shot can be taken as the birds are coming down, the lead picture should be established below the selected target, but not too far below in most cases. It is a mistake to start the gun above the bird and swing the muzzle down through it. If the gun is mounted and the muzzle is over the target, the bird will be blocked out by the muzzle. It is better to bring the muzzle to the leading edge of the descending bird and establish a lead picture under it. It is critical to maintain a focus on the target and not stop the gun.

Once a hunter's movement is detected by the bird, it will usually change it's flight path and begin to ascend quickly. The leading edge focus should change to the head of the bird, and the muzzle can be brought either slightly under or into the bird to start the shot sequence. With the target in focus, the muzzle is then moved to the desired lead picture and the shot is taken. Keep in mind that you will have more time than you think, and getting the visual focus and proper insertion point will be critical to success.

Diver ducks are a different breed altogether. Instead of taking off vertically, divers run across the water until airborne. They tend to prefer open water and they usually feed on vegetation or shellfish found under the water's surface, often to depths of 20 feet or more.

Most divers have a fast wing beat, and when coming in to a decoy spread they appear to rush in to the rig instead of descending into it. This flight characteristic is a major factor that separates diver hunting and puddle duck hunting. Since divers prefer open water, hunting for them is often done from stilt blinds in shallow bays or from layout boats surrounded by decoys.

The sea duck species like eiders and scoters are large, hardy birds with a very thick coating of down to keep them warm in the harsh conditions in which they live. As a result, most sea duck hunters use either 12 or 10 gauge guns with large shot to cleanly harvest these birds.

They are often hunted from shore blinds around shellfish beds in coastal regions. They tend to congregate large flocks on the water, but will readily decoy to an attractive spread. Sea duck hunters

(left) The rewards of good calling and shooting can mean three limits of greenheads. Here are the author and Dr. Mike Passaglia after a great morning at the famous Live Oak Gun Club in the Butte Sink region of northern California. Not shown – Bob Lashinsky.

(below) Argentina has tremendous waterfowl hunting. These Magellan geese were taken in Buenos Aires province.

When ducks are passing by, you will usually need to give them a bit of lead, even if they are over your decoys.

don't usually call to the birds to attract them. They leave that job up to their decoys, and since the drake eider ducks are primarily white, a number of those types of decoys are usually included in a spread.

Since most sea ducks are fairly large birds and typically fly low over the water, they can present the shooter with a variety of challenges. First of all the size of these birds often make it difficult to judge their range from the gun. As a result, it is smart to properly gauge the distance to the most distant decoy and take shots only within that range.

The size can also betray the read on the speed of the bird. Large birds are often traveling much faster than they appear, and since most of these birds will be taken either crossing or decoying, lead pictures will usually have to be seen. Since they fly low over the water, it will be easy to shoot over them if the insertion of the muzzle doesn't get on line with the bird as the gun is mounted.

Many shot presentations at diver ducks and sea ducks are similar to those of overhead or passing puddle ducks. The presentation angle of such shots is more crossing, so they take a visible lead to be successful. These birds can be traveling at speeds of 40 to 60 miles per hour. In some instances that speed is even greater. As a result, the forward lead required to hit such targets can be significant.

If the birds are in fairly close, any of the prescribed shooting methods can be used. If they are at a distance of 35 or more yards, some form of pull away or maintained lead will work best.

Goose hunting is actually quite different from duck hunting. The birds are bigger and they appear to be flying at a much slower speed than they really are. Most of the time shooters are either in a pit blind or laying down in a decoy spread when hunting geese, and the visual perspective from ground level is certainly different than it is

from a seated or standing position above ground.

When shooting decoying geese, the leads are not nearly what they are when the birds are taken passing. On most landing geese, just get the gun into the bird on the leading edge or direction it is traveling. Keep it moving with the bird and pull forward to the lead you think will get the job done.

Shooting passing geese is much more complicated process. Because of the size of the birds, many hunters have trouble determining the distance of the shot. And because geese are capable of flying up to around 60 miles per hour, the leads at distance are significant.

Since most of the goose species are large in size, they appear to be flying much slower at a distance than they actually are. As a result, the lead

Geese don't like to see high objects in their landing area, so most goose hunting is done from layout or pit blinds.

picture for a successful shot of often more than most hunters think. Some goose species from beak to tail are three to four feet in distance, and that distance alone is enough to confuse a lead picture.

When shooting passing geese, try focusing on the head of the bird. Move the gun so that the insertion point starts at least at the head if not slightly forward of that. This will help insure a visible lead picture, which will be needed on long passing shots.

Waterfowl hunting is truly a traditional sport in many parts of the world. Because of the different sizes and speeds of the waterfowl species, it is a real challenge for a hunter to become an excellent shot on all of them. But shooting is shooting, and proper focus and technique will go a long way toward your success.

Geese taken on a rainy October morning near Clair, Saskatchewan.

Hunting the Uplands

It's a safe bet that more shotgunners worldwide venture afield in search of the upland bird species than any other. It's pretty easy to see why when you consider how many species are classified as upland birds. The traditional upland species include pheasant, grouse, quail and partridge. Surprisingly two birds that you might not consider as upland birds, the dove and turkey, are also classified as such.

We've taken the time to discuss the shooting styles that might best apply on the upland species, and we've even talked about how to hunt behind pointing and flushing dogs. So let's take a look at the various species of upland birds to disclose some of their distinct characteristics that might give you a bit of an edge in the field.

PHEASANTS

If there is a more beautiful sight in upland gunning than a majestic ringneck pheasant rooster busting cover over a well-trained dog, I cannot imagine what it could be. The ringneck pheasant is not a native bird to North America. The species was introduced to various parts of the U.S. and Canada in the late 1800s by a government envoy to China, but the birds survived in the wild only in certain regions of the country. The most successful regions were in the northern tier of states along and south of the Canadian border, the far west and the upper midwest. The upper midwest states of Kansas, Iowa, Nebraska and North and South Dakota are best known as pheasant country, but other northern tier states across the country hold a huntable population of birds as well. Today there are millions of wild pheasants in those regions of both countries.

Like many upland birds, the pheasant is susceptible to adverse weather changes that affect not only its breeding habits, but also its ability to survive. For the birds to thrive in an area they need adequate food, moisture and habitat. If any of these necessities if missing in a given year, the pheasant crop for that season will be adversely affected. Fortunately these birds bounce back quickly with good conditions, and a poor hatch one year can be reversed quickly the next.

There are many ways to hunt the elusive ringneck, but one thing is certain. You'll have to hunt him on the run because he's a bird that would rather run from danger than fly. And since you need to get him airborne to make a clean harvest, here are some of the more popular techniques for hunting the ringneck pheasant.

Probably the most accepted methods of hunting pheasants in North America are hunting them over pointing or flushing dogs and push and block. Both of these methods are very effective when planned properly, and can be exercised with one or more shooters.

When hunting pheasants, it's best to hunt into the wind. There a couple of reasons for this. First of all the birds prefer to flush into the wind, and when you walk into the wind, the chances of the birds hearing your approach is minimized. And you can bet that wild birds can hear your approach. In fact, it's not uncommon for roosters to flush when you drive into a field or close a truck door once the season starts.

Hunting into the wind will also give the dogs a chance to scent the birds before they get to them. You will want the dogs to work as slowly as possible and cover as much of an area as possible because many a smart rooster has survived by holding tight until both dogs and hunters passed by.

In most instances, however, the pheasant will run ahead of the dogs until cornered or pressured to the point of indecision. Once the bird holds, the dog should indicate so by either pointing or working more deliberately before flushing the bird.

The majority of shots you will encounter when hunting over dogs will be on birds flushing away from the gun. These straight away and quartering shots do not require much lead, regardless of the distance the bird is from the gun. As a result, the swing through style or a form of modified pull away will work best, and the speed of the bird will dictate the speed of the muzzle as you take the shot.

The most important aspect of shooting a flushing bird is to take the extra half second to actually focus on the bird. If possible, transfer the focus to the head of the bird since it's very possible to miss behind a flushing cock bird that can be as much as three feet long from head to tail. That's a lot of target surface to focus on, and a narrowed focus

Hunters find pheasant hunting both challenging and exciting.

A good bird dog can make life much easier for the upland hunter.

will always be better than trying to use the entire bird as your intended target. If possible, try looking at the white ring around the rooster's neck.

A second reason to let the eyes work for you is that when hunting wild birds, you can only shoot roosters. The colorful birds are easy to pick out with the light conditions are favorable, but you've really got to look closely when shooting in certain light conditions. When hunting with a buddy or a group of hunters, it is common for them to call out "rooster" or "hen" when birds flush. This is very helpful when light conditions make the birds hard to identify.

The push and block method is very popular in the American upper midwest and on traditional driven shoots in the British Isles and Europe. This method utilizes hunters or beaters who move through a designated area pushing the birds to one or more shooters who have positioned themselves in a location to intercept the birds moving ahead of the pushers.

It is important for the blockers to move slowly, as they will walk past birds that elect to hold tight until the danger passes. In many instances moving slowly will make the birds nervous and will force them to flush, giving the pushers an opportunity for a shot.

If the pusher numbers are not sufficient to cover a large block, try zig zagging left and right to cover more ground laterally. This can be effective as it gives the impression of a larger number of pushers moving through an area.

The blockers at the end of the block being pushed will not typically get much action until the pushers get within 50 or so yards. Birds running on the ground ahead of them will be trapped between the pushers and the blockers, and will be forced to try to escape by flying. Needless to say, the action can get pretty heated since some blocks of land hold large numbers of birds.

In most cases the shots presented to the blockers will be either crossing or driven, and the shooting styles used to hit them consistently are somewhat different from those used on flushing targets. Because the angle of the shots presented require more lead to hit them, shooting styles like pull away and maintained lead will probably mean more consistent kills. Rest assured that when a hunter is in a blocking position in a field full of pheasants, the action can be fast and furious, and the shots presented will be very similar to those taken while shooting doves. So if you use the shooting styles that work well on flushing pheasants while blocking, chances are pretty good that your average bird per shot will suffer. Remember that the presentation angle usually dictates which shooting style works best on a given shot.

When hunting alone or with a buddy or two and no dog, you've got to be patient. Use the zig-zag pattern as you move through your hunting area, and walk slowly. Many wary roosters will simply squat down and let you pass if you're in a hurry, but they often get nervous and flush when you move slowly.

Small groups will have a tough time hemming up birds in a big field, but there are lots of smaller areas that can be effectively hunted with one to three or four hunters. Old farmsteads, wind rows, plumb thickets and ditch banks should be hunted thoroughly since they provide excellent resting and roosting cover. If you find such areas near water or a grain field that the birds might use for feeding, you've possibly found the mother lode. Hunt patiently and you've got a real chance for success.

QUAIL

There are a number of quail species found throughout the world, but we're going to focus on those species found in America and northern Mexico. You can bet that there are significant differences between the most hunted of the quail species, the Bobwhite, and the other quail species found primarily in the arid, dry states in the western U.S. Quail are not migratory, so they have to be creatures of their individual habitat.

The Bobwhite quail is a gamebird that is found in number of different climates. He is common in the eastern two thirds of the U.S. and in the northeastern region of Mexico. The Bobwhite is a covey bird, so it's not uncommon to flush 10 to 25 birds at a time.

The Bobwhite is at home in agricultural areas

Quail hunting in the Deep South is much more than shooting birds. Mule drawn wagons, guides on horseback, fabulous dogs and a group of friends are ingredients for a great day in the field.

where adequate nesting and roosting cover exist. As is the case with all gamebirds and animals, the availability of habitat and water is the key to sustaining huntable populations. These things are so important that Bobwhite populations can fluctuate significantly from year to year depending on the habitat and moisture conditions in their home area.

Unlike the quail of the arid west, Bobwhites would rather try to hide than run from perceived danger. As a result, they are more easily hunted with pointing dogs. Bobwhites will usually hold for a point, although birds that have experienced hunting pressure before will be somewhat more wary.

When flushed, a Bobwhite covey erupts from the ground with what many hunters might consider a thunderous roar or whirring wings. The birds have no definitive flight plan, but they will fly to the deepest cover they can find. Their only thought is survival. The flush of a wild Bobwhite

Few birds are more handsome than "Gentleman Bob."

covey can be very confusing to even the most seasoned of hunters, as shots from many angles are presented.

The experienced gun knows the value of picking his targets on a covey rise one at a time. Once the eyes lock on a bird, it will be important to stay focused on that bird, since it is possible that other birds in the covey could also come into the shooter's view. In many instances hunters will harvest two or more birds on a single shot when focusing on only one bird, but it's rare to harvest more than one bird with a single shot if you are trying to do so.

The vast majority of shots on Bobwhites will be either straight away from the gun or at some quartering angle. As a result, visible lead pictures

When faced with a wild covey rise, the first thing you've got to do is pick out one bird to take.

are not usually needed to harvest birds. And since the shots are usually going away from the gun, hunters often have much more time to take a shot than they might think. You will find that by taking the time to actually pick a single target and focus on it, you will be able to harvest more birds with much less stress.

You will find that many birds are missed because the hunter shoots too fast. Remember that, when shooting, you'll want to take your eyes to the target first and your hands and the gun to the target second. Remember, too, that the position of the gun muzzle before the flush is very important. If you can minimize the muzzle movement, you'll likely bag more birds with fewer shots.

Even though the Bobwhite is often found feeding in grain fields, his home habitat usually includes wooded areas. As a result, many of the little birds are flushed in open forests, which can drive hunters just about nuts. Obstacles such as tall bushes and trees will tend to distract hunters as the birds take flight. It is always best to survey your surroundings before walking in on a point. In other words, make sure you know where your

shooting windows are and where your hunting partners are. Try to determine where you think the birds might go when flushed, which means think like a quail if you can. Keep in mind that wild birds will tend to go to the deepest cover they can once flushed.

For the most part, shots at Bobwhite quail are usually taken at pretty close range. It is uncommon for shots to be more than 35 yards, so hunters should use the best choke/load combination possible at close to medium distances for their gun of choice. When hunting wild Bobwhites, most guns will choose number seven and a half or eight shot in a light to medium velocity load. The Bobwhite is a thin-skinned bird, so a high velocity load is not as important as one that patterns well at the distances where shots are being taken.

Since most of the shots on Bobwhites are fairly close, more open chokes are usually preferred. In many settings skeet and improved cylinder chokes are perfect for two barrel guns, while the improved cylinder tube is preferred for single barrel actions.

WESTERN QUAIL SPECIES

As mentioned earlier, there is a significant difference between the Bobwhite quail and the different species of western quail. The species of quails found in the western states of the U.S. and northwest Mexico (blue, California or valley, scaled, Gambel's, Mearn' and elegante) are truly creatures of their habitat. Like the pheasant, they prefer to run to cover rather than fly to it. There are a couple of reasons for this.

First of all, protective habitat is tough to come by where these birds live. The arid west doesn't offer much tree cover, and the sparse, low bushy vegetation isn't thick enough for the birds to fly and land just anywhere. Second, the lack of vegetative cover could mean that the birds once flushed, would be exposed for longer periods of time to predators from above. Hawks, falcons and eagles find flushed birds that have to fly long distances to reach cover easy prey. As a result, the western species of quails would much rather run to cover than fly.

The very rare Elegante quail is only found in northwestern Mexico and southern Arizona.

These species are found in coveys of all sizes, and because of their tendency to run when being pursued by hunters or dogs, the coveys may be spread out over a wider area than you might find when hunting the Bobwhite species. When walking in behind dogs on point, be prepared for flushes from not only from where the dogs indicate the birds might be, but from cover nearby as well.

Because these species tend to run rather than hold, you might find yourself in continuous pursuit of a covey. Once pressured enough, the birds will often flush while being pushed. Obviously you must be ready to take a shot at anytime once the birds have been located. Since you will likely be moving often before the shot, make sure of your footing and your surroundings as you move to the birds.

Since the western quail species will not hold for a point like the Bobwhite, you might want to consider using a little more choke in your gun. Most shooters will use size seven and a half shot and medium velocity loads for western quail, and some guns even opt for number six shot for their second or third shot. A good choke choice would be improved cylinder, with either a light modified or modified choke for the second barrel. When shooting a semi-auto or pump action, a light modified choke offers an excellent compromise.

HUNGARIAN PARTRIDGE AND CHUKAR

North America wingshooters are fortunate to have two old world partridge species to pursue each fall. The Hungarian partridge and chukar partridge are both recent immigrants to our continent, and both of them have found our shores to their liking.

Less than 100 years ago, the European gray partridge was being introduced to various regions of North America. History books tell us that the partridge didn't do so well in some areas, but it did seem to thrive in the southern regions of the Canadian province of Alberta. The birds that seemed to adapt best to southern Alberta's habitat and climatic conditions were brought to the area from the plains of Hungary. As a result, the bird became known as the Hungarian partridge.

One of the premier upland species is the Hungarian partridge. These birds were taken in western Colorado.

(above) **Few gamebirds are more beautiful than the wild ringneck pheasant.**

the Atlantic provinces of Canada and down into New York state.

The hun is a covey bird that is about twice the size of the Bobwhite quail. Huns do not naturally thrive in heavily treed habitats, and are found in native grasslands and around agricultural fields. For that reason, huns survive much better in the west than in the east.

The hun is an exciting bird to hunt, since they will hold for a pointing dog and are strong flyers when flushed. They tend to flush more vertically than do the quail or grouse species, so shooters often have more time to pick a target and take a shot than they might think.

Early in the hunting season, hun coveys usu-

The Hungarian partridge, or hun as it is affectionately known, proved to be an very adaptable species. They are at home in the lush farmlands found west of the Mississippi River and in the dry wheat fields in prairie Canada. Over the past few decades, Hungarian partridge populations have expanded into the province of Saskatchewan and the northern tier of U.S. states such as Oregon, Washington, Montana and the Dakotas. There are other pockets of populations in the upper midwest,

ally consist of two adult birds and their surviving young from the season's hatch. Covey size is dependent on habitat conditions, and in a good habitat year finding coveys of 12 to 16 birds is possible. Huns don't need a visible water source to survive. They get their water from dew drops found on their food source.

Like so many gamebirds, the hun is a creature of habit. It is very active early in the morning and from mid-afternoon until it's time to go to roost. When hunting huns it makes sense to take these facts into consideration.

Wild huns will hold for a point, but not for an extended period of time after the hunting season has gotten underway. When hunting huns, it is important to get to the point quickly and be ready for a thunderous flush because the birds will all flush at once. There's really no need to look for singles, because when one bird goes, the rest do too. Keep a sharp eye on the birds as they fly and glide away from the gun. The birds tend to fly together and if you can see them down, there's a chance that you can flush the covey again.

Unlike the pheasant, huns will not seek cover to let the danger walk by. They are a smaller bird

The first thing you've got to do when a pheasant flushes in front of you is identify hen or rooster when hunting wild birds. This hen happens to be on a hunting preserve, so she's fair game.

than the pheasant, so it makes more sense for them to fly from sparse cover. Keep this in mind when hunting around field edges. You'll likely find the birds out in the field or in thin weed patches rather than thick grass.

Many hunters are startled at the flush of a partridge covey because the birds are capable of reaching top speed in a very short distance. It's important not to approach a covey of huns with the expectation of harvesting more than one bird on the flush. While doing so is certainly possible, taking the birds one at a time is the best way to go.

Most of the shots will be quartering away when shooting huns, so rushing the shot is not necessary. Since the birds will often flush 20 to 25 yards in front of the gun, a slightly tighter choke might be in order. A good combination would be light modified and modified in a double gun or light mod early in the season and mod later on in a single barrel gun. Most shooters prefer size seven and a half for huns, but on windy days sixes could be a good choice.

The chukar is also classified as a partridge, but it thrives in a habitat that is very different from its Hungarian cousin. The chukar, which was introduced to North America in the 1930s, survived much better in the arid mountain landscape

Wild chukars are a bird of the arid western states. Occasionally you can find them around sage brush, but most of the time they're near rocky outcroppings in mountainous areas.

The chukar is also found on many hunting preserves throughout America.

of the western states in America. The birds that thrived were from the dry hills of India. In Europe the chukar is known as the red-legged partridge, where it is revered by wingshooters as a true test of their shotgunning skills. And had the stock of birds come from Europe instead of India, the chukar may have been more of a farmland bird.

When hunting wild chukars, hunters probably feel like they are part mountain goat, because these birds are usually found on rocky hillsides or grassy slopes. They must have a water source for survival, so finding such a habitat in the west will often produce a number of birds.

Like their Hungarian counterparts they are somewhat predictable in their daily routine. They feed early in the morning and late in the afternoon. At some point they will go to water, often after each feeding session. They'll loaf around a rocky shelf and out of the wind in the middle of the day. So if you can outwit the chukar by understanding his habits, you might have a leg up on your hunting peers.

Chukars are covey birds and are very vocal. As a result they can give away their location easily. But one thing's for sure. A flighted wild chukar flying and gliding down a hillside is a very challenging target.

Chukars are larger in size than the Hungarian partridge, so most hunters choose 20 gauge or larger guns fueled by a good load of number six or seven and a half shot. Wild chukars can be pretty wary, so many shots are in the 30 plus yard range. They will run ahead of the gun when being pursued, especially in the open rocky areas of their habitat, and they can flush at any time. As a result, choke selection should be limited to modified or even improved modified as the season progresses.

GROUSE

Few gamebirds generate more excitement and passion in a wingshooter than the various species grouse found throughout the North American continent. The vast majority of dedicated grouse hunters are serious in their search of the ruffed grouse, which is found in much of the eastern two thirds of the U.S. from the north Georgia border to the Canadian border, and in the southern sections of much of Canada. The western grouse species, such as sharptail, blue, spruce and sage species, along with greater and lesser prairie chickens, are located in the great plains states and in the mountain west. There are also a couple of species of ptarmigan found primarily in Arctic Canada, Alaska and the high elevations of the Colorado Rockies.

RUFFED GROUSE

If you ever took the time to categorize bird hunters, the ruffed grouse enthusiast would likely have his own following. For the hunter who avidly pursues the ruffed grouse, no other game bird or animal can provide the same thrill and excitement. For many bird hunters, matching wits with the ruffed grouse is the ultimate wingshooting challenge.

The ruffed grouse is the most widespread of the grouse species found in North America. It's range extends from Alaska through the West Coast states, across the mountain states, through the midwest and then eastward to the Atlantic Provinces of Canada. They are found in the wild as far south as the hills of north Georgia. The bird's coloration varies from gray to brown depending on the region.

But what is it that makes this bird so difficult to hunt? There are many theories as to why the ruffed grouse just might be our smartest and most elusive gamebird. When market hunting was a common practice in the eastern U.S., the ruffed grouse was in big demand at restaurants.

Grouse and woodcock are often found in similar habitat. These birds were taken at Leen's Lodge in Maine.

Its white meat and succulent flavor made it so. In many areas a pair of grouse would fetch $.50 to $.75, which was good money at the time.

There's no doubt that hunting pressure and the presence of man contributed to the ruffed grouse's ghost-like evolution. This has to be a major reason since grouse found in remote wilderness areas of Canada are easily taken by simply walking up to the tree they are perched in and plinking them out with a .22 rifle. Don't forget that the Indians had no trouble harvesting grouse with rocks or bows and arrows.

It's pretty tough to get that close to the ruffed grouse in huntable areas these days, especially when hunting them with a pointing dog. In fact, many hunts are based on flushes counted rather than birds harvested. Many hunters will swear that a flushed grouse has the uncanny ability to position a tree between itself and the gun just at the right time to help it escape. The likely truth is that the grouse's habitat and ability to fly through the thinnest of openings in the forest probably contribute more to his ability to escape than anything else.

Since the bird is so adept at giving hunters the slip, it might help to understand his habitat and tendencies in order to get a leg up on Mr. Ruff. He is a non-migratory bird who lives in forests and woodlands, especially open woods and cutover areas.

Most grouse hunters hunt the old road beds, trails and logging roads where there are open grassy areas allowing sunshine to the forest floor. Fallen trees are a favorite hideout as are logs in an open woodland which the cock bird will use as a drumming site. Drumming is the grouse's way of attracting a female bird for mating season.

The ruffed grouse's diet consists of about ten percent insect and ninety percent vegetative matter. He simply loves chokeberries and cranberries, and if you can find an apple orchard, you'll probably find grouse. He'll also dine on the buds of birch, aspen and hemlock trees. Keep in mind that he's not a bird that is comfortable in dense woods. He prefers a more open environment, although when flushed, he has the ability to make any environment look cluttered to the hunter.

The grouse seems to sense when hunting season is on, and when pressured he can be tough to find. Grouse can be hunted with a dog, and many hunters opt for a flushing breed that will work close and slow to the gun. In most cases hunting slowly and quietly works best, but be ready for anything. The coloration of the ruffed grouse renders it virtually invisible when on the ground, so it's possible to walk close to a bird who thinks that if he sits still the danger will pass.

On the flush, the bird explodes from cover with a loud whirring of wings. In most cases you'll only have a few yards to act. Of course the most important thing to do is actually find the bird visually. You'll have a bit more time than you think if you can focus on the bird and move as he moves.

Rarely is the time when a shooter actually sees a definable lead picture on a flushing grouse. More often than not, the move of the gun is a poke and a prayer, but you'll be surprised how many birds you'll bag if you are focused on your target. Grouse are much like woodcock. They don't tend to give you much time to take a shot. But whatever time they do give you, make sure you use it all!

The ruffed grouse is a decent sized bird, about one and a half to two pounds in weight. But it's not that difficult to bring one down. As a result, many grouse hunters opt for a short barreled, lightweight 12 or 20 gauge model and a medium load of number six or seven and a half shot. Many hunters use a double gun with a fairly open choke for the first barrel and no more than a modified tube for the second. It's pretty rare to get a crack at a ruffed grouse more than 30 yards away.

The action is close, fast and furious, and when a grouse hunter fills a limit on Mr. Ruff, he can drive home with his head held high.

SHARPTAIL GROUSE AND PRAIRIE CHICKENS

It's pretty easy to lump these two grouse species together, because their range and the techniques to hunt them are so similar. The sharptail grouse is a native of the grasslands and prairies from southern Canadian provinces of Alberta and

Saskatchewan and western states like Montana, the Dakotas, Nebraska, Minnesota, Wisconsin and Colorado. The prairie chicken's range is more restricted, with populations found in South Dakota, Nebraska, Oklahoma, Texas and New Mexico.

The sharptail is appropriately named, as it is differentiated from the prairie chicken by its pointed tail. It is the only North American grouse species with such a tail configuration. The prairie chicken has a short, rounded tail. The sharptail's coloration is a bit lighter than that of the prairie chicken, but other than these few differences, they are pretty much the same bird.

Where they are very similar is in the difficulty of hunting them. They are flock birds, and it's common for one or more of the birds to have sentry duty. Getting close to them in their grassland habitat is difficult, so many shots taken at these birds are from a good distance.

If you plan to hunt these birds with a dog, it's best to use one of the pointing breeds. A pointer working into the wind can pick up scent without pushing the birds too fast, but a flushing dog could move the birds more quickly causing a flush at full choke distance.

These grouse tend to weigh a couple of pounds, so hunters will want to use enough choke and shell to get the job done. Keep in mind that their chosen habitat is grassland prairie, so most flushes will take place well in front of the gun.

Since getting close to the birds can be a challenge, most hunters opt for a 12 gauge with heavy field loads or 20 gauge gun with one of the small magnum loads available. Choke selection ranges from modified to full for most hunters since 40 yard shots are fairly common. The pellet size of choice seems to be number six, but later in the season, many hunters move to fours. Fortunately the birds fly and land together, so keeping an eye on them may give you another opportunity.

BLUE GROUSE

The blue grouse is a popular gamebird. It is a fairly large bird that can weigh up to around three pounds. It's range overlaps that of the ruffed grouse in some western states. Blue grouse prefer a more open woodland habitat than do ruffed grouse, so hunt in cut over forests, on the edge of streams and areas with green grasses or berry and fruit producing bushes and trees.

The blue grouse is a strong flyer, and it flushes with a roar of its large wings. The blue grouse flies about the same speed as the ruffed grouse, but since it is often flying downhill in its habitat, the speed might seem even faster. Needless to say, a three pound blue grouse rocketing downhill is no easy target.

The birds are found in flocks and can easily be hunted with pointing or flushing dogs. In wilderness areas they border on stupid as they have no fear of man. But in areas where hunting them is common, they provide a exhilarating wingshooting challenge. When you consider where the blue grouse lives, you can understand why you'd better be in good physical shape before heading out for a day in the grouse woods.

Early in the season, the birds will hold for a dog much better than they will when they've been hunted for a few weeks. As a result, choke, gun and load selection are a matter of personal choice depending on how you plan to hunt. Because of the size of the birds, shot size should be limited to four, five or six. Any gun 20 gauge or larger will get the job done, and most hunters tend to use modified chokes when hunting blue grouse.

The birds are migratory, as they move from the mountains to the valley floor and back up again. But during the hunting season, you'll find them near water and in open wooded and grassy areas in the high country. The best time to hunt the blue grouse is mid-morning and mid-afternoon. They usually don't start feeding until the dew has dried off of the grassy leaves in their habitat.

The western states offers some great grouse hunting. Blue grouse, sharptail grouse and prairie chickens are found in many areas of the west and upper midwest. This blue grouse was taken near Meeker, Colorado.

Hunting in the west can be a challenge. This chukar was pointed and shot in western Colorado.

PTARMIGAN

There are two main ptarmigan species found in North America – the rock ptarmigan, which inhabits the western Rocky Mountains and the more abundant willow ptarmigan, which is found in Arctic Canada and Alaska. The willow ptarmigan is much the same bird that shooters in Scotland hold in such reverence, but it's not a difficult bird to hunt in North America.

Perhaps the most intriguing thing about the ptarmigan is its ability to change color to adapt to its surroundings. The birds are a beautiful brown and black with a bit of white in the summer when their tundra habitat explodes in all the colors of the rainbow. As winter approaches, the birds turn solid white to offer them protection from predators as the snows of the Arctic north begin to fall.

The willow ptarmigan migrates a few hundred miles each year during the late fall to escape the sub-zero conditions that are common in its habitat. But before they migrate, they present hunters with a wonderful hunting experience. It's not necessary to use a pointing or flushing dog to hunt them, but in the tundra wilderness of Alaska and Canada, a good dog will save the hunter a great deal of walking.

The willow ptarmigan can be found in abundance where they find water, dwarf willow bushes with the succulent leaves and wild cranberries and bear berries that make up their diet. In most tundra regions where the birds are found, they show little fear of man. So vast is the tundra, that many birds have never seen a hunter.

The birds are usually found in flocks of eight to 15 birds. When flushed their flight is fairly straight away from the gun, and the predominance of white feathers on their wings make them very visible to the hunter.

Willow ptarmigan can easily be taken with 20 and 28 gauge guns. A light field load of six or seven and a half shot is more than sufficient. Because

After hunting upland birds in thick cover all morning, a lunch break can be welcomed by all.

(left) One of the most challenging birds to harvest is the helmeted guinea fowl in South Africa. These birds have great vision, so it's tough to get close to them. They fly like a wild pheasant and shooting them driven is quite a challenge.

the tundra can be a windy place, improved cylinder and modified chokes will be best, even though many of the shots presented on the flush could be taken with a skeet choke. The extra choke will help hold the pattern together in the high tundra winds.

The rock ptarmigan is similar to its cousin, but is found in huntable numbers only in a small region of the Rocky Mountains. In such terrain, these birds can be a challenge to hunt, and a dog can be a real ally.

Many shooters will use either a 12 or 20 gauge gun when hunting the rock ptarmigan, again because of the difficulties of hunting in such terrain. Getting close to the rock ptarmigan can be tough, and the shots when presented can be uphill or downhill, which can prove problematic to many hunters.

WOODCOCK

Like the ruffed grouse, the woodcock, or timberdoodle as he is affectionately called, is a gamebird with a dedicated following. Woodcock will rest and roost in many of the same habitats as the grouse,

If you spend any time hunting birds in South America, there's a good chance you'll hunt the perdiz over pointing dogs. These birds constantly relocate, driving hunter and dog crazy. They are solitary, so only look for one bird to flush at a time.

but prefer to dine on worms in damp, wetland areas instead of on leaves and berries.

The woodcock is a migratory bird that travels a north/south corridor that rivals that of many duck and goose species. It is hunted all along it migratory journey, but most diehard woodcock hunters live in the northeast section of the U.S. or the southern gulf coast states, especially Lousiana.

Because of the vegetative state of the woodcock's habitat, it's best to hunt them with a good pointing dog. Many dedicated woodcock hunters use one of the spaniel breeds because of size and tendency to hunt slowly. A woodcock is perfectly camouflaged for the forest floor, and without a good dog it's likely you would walk past a large number of birds.

When flushed the woodcock makes a whistling sound with its wings, and can fly twisting and turning away from the gun or almost vertically in an effort to escape through the tree canopy. It won't typically fly very far before landing, so it is often possible to relocate a bird that might have escaped a shot. But make sure that you don't run straight to the bird. Give him a few minutes to settle down, and he can be easily pointed again.

The woodcock is a fairly solitary bird, and it's rare to flush more than a single bird at a time. And when he does flush, you'd better be ready for just about anything. The woodcock may not be quite as adept as a ruffed grouse at putting an obstacle between himself and the gun, but you can bet they'll make fools out of the best of shotgunners.

The vast majority of shots on woodcock are quite close. As a result, small gauge guns loaded with number eight or nine shot and open chokes are the ticket. Most woodcock hunters prefer short barreled guns because of the close quarters the

One of the more difficult wingshooting challenges is the South African rock pigeon. They fly in flocks that can turn 90 degrees at high speed in unison.

little bird forces them to hunt in. Like the grouse, the timberdoodle doesn't often give you much time to shoot once he decides to flush. But if you want to be successful, make sure you use all of the time he gives you.

You'll find that you've got more time than you think if you can visually focus on the bird as he launches skyward. Since your hand speed will be faster than the bird in most cases, virtually no lead is needed to hit the bird. More often than not, just getting the gun to the bird and keeping it moving for a follow through will be enough to put the bird in the bag. But because of the usual tightness of the shot windows it's easy to stop the swing. By staying in the gun to watch the bird fall, you'll minimize your gun stopping and increase your bag.

The woodcock is a nocturnal feeder, so the best time to hunt him is early morning. He'll likely

With limited exception, most upland gunning is in open territory, so make sure you are physically ready for the demands of hunting in this kind of territory.

still be feeding at first light. An hour or so after the sun rises, you'll start to find him in his loafing and resting cover. In either case, he will hold for a pointing dog, which should provide you some exciting shooting.

Hunters worldwide are blessed with a wide variety of upland species to hunt. This book has discussed a few of the more popular species found in North America, but there are many, many more species that can be hunted. There are many species of perdiz, Francolin and guinea fowl found around the world. And just like those upland species of the Americas, they are actively pursued by upland bird enthusiasts.

Hunting the Uplands | **195**

Mastering the Mental Game

One problem with hunting in such open country is that birds can be found anywhere. A good dog like this Labrador Retriever who can find, flush and retrieve your birds is important.

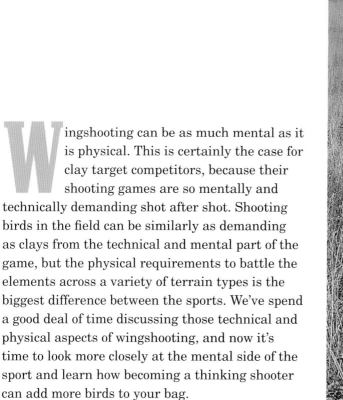

Wingshooting can be as much mental as it is physical. This is certainly the case for clay target competitors, because their shooting games are so mentally and technically demanding shot after shot. Shooting birds in the field can be similarly as demanding as clays from the technical and mental part of the game, but the physical requirements to battle the elements across a variety of terrain types is the biggest difference between the sports. We've spend a good deal of time discussing those technical and physical aspects of wingshooting, and now it's time to look more closely at the mental side of the sport and learn how becoming a thinking shooter can add more birds to your bag.

Even though we were blessed with good instinctive abilities that allow us to react to most shots that we see in the field, the best wingshooters take a mental approach to the shot before they commit the gun to the shoulder. They have learned that just throwing the gun in the direction of bird will result in marginal success at best, so getting the brain involved with its knowledge of the shooting task at hand will increase the chances of making a good shot.

The mental advantages we are talking about

Once down in a blind, make sure you can see the birds without being seen.

When the birds commit you your setup, let them get in range before making your move.

come from what we have learned about the mechanical and technical aspects of our individual shooting as well as what we know about the birds we are hunting. Consider that any good deer hunter would never venture afield without first having done some scouting to pick his hunting spot carefully. This choice of location is based on the information he can gather about the times and places his quarry might appear. It is also based on the comfort level of his shooting ability and his knowledge of the game he is hunting and its habits.

The experienced bird hunter likewise draws from his understanding of the characteristics and habits of the birds he hunts, and he recognizes his shooting limitations so that he attempts shots that are within the boundaries of his ability. When a hunter spends quality time learning as much as he can about the type of hunting he will be doing, he will undoubtedly be more prepared for the shots when they come than one who simply shows up to hunt.

LEARN THE CHARACTERISTICS OF THE BIRDS YOU HUNT

There are, of course, some things common to almost all bird hunting, whether upland or waterfowl, and it's often been said "to hunt ducks successfully, learn to think like a duck or to hunt pheasants with success, learn to think like a pheasant." While this sounds a bit goofy, it may in fact be one of the most astute comments ever made about hunting our fine feathered friends.

Most hunters know that birds generally take off and land into the wind, much like an airplane. As a result, waterfowl blinds are usually built to accommodate prevailing winds found during the hunting season at the blind location. For instance, if the prevailing winds in an area were North to Northwest during the duck season, hunters would

It's pretty easy to see which of these hunters is ready for the flush and which one is not. The hunter on the left shows great form.

be wise to face their blinds to the South or Southeast. If they want to cheat the sun a bit to allow better visibility throughout the morning, a bit more to the Southwest would work. If you don't have a directional preference, set the blind North/South to take advantage of the sun location for morning or afternoon hunts.

Waterfowlers also know that landing birds have to change direction to get away from where they were when the first shot was taken. By taking the first shot just before the birds land, the shooter will assure himself of additional time to take second and third shots if necessary.

Upland bird hunters have their little bits of information that help them bag more game too. They know the habits of pheasants, quail, partridge and grouse, and they understand that power lines or exposed limbs of trees in a dove field are a natural draw to the speedy birds. And don't forget that the flushing species will generally take off into the wind, too, so working into the wind will provide the best results.

The mental process in bird hunting is based on the shooter being able to put this information to work while in the field, so that he will be prepared for virtually any type of shooting situation. This means paying attention to things like the wind, the sun, how the dogs are working and noticing when they appear to be birdy, and getting the gun positioned over the dogs and safely above the horizon in preparation of the flush. It means making a plan on how to take a bird after watching it fly across a 50 acre field towards a shooting location.

And it means being ready for action when driving to the blockers at the end of a corn field leads to a sky filled with brilliantly colored cock pheasants. And finally, it means that you have to be able to commit to a shot and have some idea of how you want to take the bird. In other words, wingshooting is not all instinctive. There's much more to it than simply throwing the gun skyward and pulling the trigger.

This preparation is critical to a shooter's success in the field. As a result, many shooters who

When it comes to a successful flush and shot, the hunters and dogs must ultimately work as a team.

stumble along aimlessly with the gun draped over the shoulder aren't really hunting because they will almost always be surprised and ultimately behind virtually every bird they see. Inevitably their major problem is not being mentally or physically ready when a shot presents itself. And in almost every case, it's a lack of mental focus on what's going on around them.

Please understand that we're not talking about having to be on our toes each and every minute of the hunt. Chances are that will take a great deal of the enjoyment out of a day afield. We only have to be conscious of safety at all times. But being aware of what is going on around us while hunting is a big part of the experience. It is also important to realize that you do have ample time to react to a bird if you can get a focus on the speed, angle and distance quickly.

If you have working knowledge of the characteristics of the birds you hunt, it gives you an advantage. If you can read the the signs of how a dog works a bird, and understand a bit about cover, wind and terrain while in the field, your chances of success will greatly improve. Once you learn to think like the bird you hunt, you will usually be

When birds flush in front of the gun, quite a few things have to happen quickly. Things like focus, mount, insertion point and lead all have meaning once the birds are up.

ready both mentally and physically to go into action when the time for a shot arrives.

Mental preparation includes more than an understanding of the habits of your quarry and how to use the land and elements to one's advantage. It also means that the shooter can make split second decisions based on what the bird is doing in flight. These decisions include the type of shooting style to be used, the speed of the gun's approach to the bird and the timing of when to take the shot.

Rest assured that it requires practice to gain experience, because it will ultimately be that experience that the shooter will draw from in virtually every shooting situation. Just remember that mental preparedness is a direct result of technique, mechanics and target focus, and there is no better teaching tool than time in the saddle. You've got to spend time afield because no where will you learn more about the birds you hunt than in a face to face encounter with them.

Safety First and Always

Adults need reminding about safety too. This safety orientation took place at the Ringneck Rance in Tipton, Kansas.

Without question, the single most important aspect of any shooting sport is safety. We have been very fortunate that hunting is statistically one of the safest of all forms of recreation, and it is the hunter's respect for his safety and those around him that make this so. When there are mistakes made in the field, they are generally caused by carelessness on the hunter's part. Unfortunately, many seasoned and experienced hunters are the ones who typically make those mistakes. That's right, the experienced gun is more likely to be careless than the novice because it is the experienced shooter who can take things for granted. You can never assume things are safe when it comes to shooting or hunting.

Fortunately there are training programs nationwide to help hunters of all levels prepare for the hunt. The Hunter Education programs in most states are generally filled with youngsters who are required to have the hunter certification card before they can hunt or buy a hunting license. But a closer look at these programs revels that a number of adult females and males take the course for the knowledge it provides.

Some states require every out of state hunter, regardless of their age, to have a hunter education certificate before they can hunt. And since the hunter education programs are open to anyone, it's a pretty good idea for shooters to attend one just to further develop their skills, safety habits and knowledge about the outdoors. It will be a show of support for the shooting sports, and shooters will gain valuable information that will help make their outdoor experience more pleasurable.

HUNTER SAFETY STARTS WITH YOU

Practicing good gun safety at home and in the field is not difficult, but it does take some effort so that it is a part of a shooter's everyday routine. Let's look at some of the safety factors that a shooter should be aware of every time they pick up or store a favorite scattergun, or any gun for that matter.

(left) You can never be too safe. This Saf-T-Plug product is a great idea for all shooters.

(below) When you pick up a gun, check the barrel for obstructions. Better safe than sorry.

When walking in the field, keeping the muzzle of a loaded gun pointed safely in an upward direction can help eliminate accidents.

ALWAYS CHECK TO MAKE SURE THE GUN IS UNLOADED

First of all, it goes without saying that every gun should be treated as if it were loaded. This statement has been around for as long as firearms have, yet accidents still happen from time to time when people take things for granted.

When a shooter picks up a shotgun, he should open the breech or chamber first to make sure that it isn't loaded until he gets to his hunting location. The same applies for when storing the gun or just casing it for travel to another hunting site. A visibly unloaded shotgun is a safe shotgun.

If you shoot a "break" gun, it is possible to carry it in the crook of the arm, with the action open until it is time to hunt. When you take a break from the hunt, make sure to break the gun open to make it safe.

Always check your shooting pouch and pockets to make sure that your ammo is proper for your gun of choice. It's easy to make a mistake with mixed gauge ammo, so make sure you check it before going afield.

CHECK FOR OBSTRUCTIONS IN THE BARREL

Another advantage to checking the bores for safety is to make sure that there are no obstructions in the barrel. Because of the intense pressures generated within the bores when a shot is fired, there can be no obstruction in the barrel whatsoever. Sometimes even the smallest piece of debris is enough to change the pressure readings in barrel and cause it to rupture, which can cause injury or death to the shooter or persons nearby.

As a result, it's a good idea to always check the bores before loading the gun for the first time, and then anytime the muzzle has touched the ground or some foreign object.

ALWAYS HAVE THE MUZZLE POINTED DOWNRANGE AND AT A SAFE ELEVATION

Once in the field and the gun is loaded, it is very important that the muzzle of the gun always be pointed safely downrange and away from other hunters. Keeping the muzzle pointed at an elevation that is clearly safe should be practiced as well. Upland bird hunters typically consider above the horizon as a safe elevation, but in open areas found in many hunting situations, the horizon can be below the shooter's eyes. In order to make sure, a safe elevation is typically somewhere between 45 and 90 degrees from the ground.

Many hunters like to carry the gun at a 45-degree angle across the body. This means that for right hand shooters the muzzle will cross the

body to the left. For left hand shooters the opposite is the case. This is a good carrying position while actually hunting birds afoot. Once the hunt is finished, a single barrel action gun should be shifted to a more vertical carrying position with the breech visibly open for transfer out of the field. Double guns should be open and placed barrels forward over the shoulder or in the crook of the arm for transport out of the field.

It's a good idea, and in some areas a law, to case the gun anytime it is being transported in a vehicle. This is the case if you plan to relocate your area while hunting as well. Any time you travel in your vehicle, the gun should be unloaded and cased or placed in a gun slip for safety.

KEEP AMMO SEPARATE

Bird hunters have a tendency to own more than one gun to accommodate the various types of birds they love to hunt, and it's not uncommon for their guns to be of different gauges. In fact many wingshooters prefer 20 gauge or smaller for most of their bird shooting.

As a result, it is possible to venture afield one day with a 12 bore and the next with a 20. The ammunition for these guns of different gauges is not interchangeable, and sometimes ammo can get mixed, especially if the hunter uses the same jacket, vest or pouch for all of his hunting. If this happens, it is possible that a shell from a smaller gauge can get lodged in the barrel of a larger bore without the hunter's knowledge. This can easily happen when the shooter gets in a hurry to load his gun.

In order to minimize the chances of an accident happening, separate clothing or containers for carrying ammo should be used. In all cases, it's proper to check what loads are in the vest, bag, etc. before venturing into the field. This will eliminate the chances of an accident occurring because of an improperly sized shell.

REMEMBER THE SAFETY CATCH PROCEDURE

For years double guns were built with automatic safeties, meaning that the safety catch would automatically reset once the breech was opened. Today, however, many hunters are venturing afield with guns made more for target shooting which don't have automatic safeties. And single barrel action shotguns, autoloaders and pumps, don't have the auto safeties either, which means that the hunter has to physically put the gun on safe after the shot has been fired.

This aspect of safety has to be made a habit, and the best way to do it is to practice it constantly. Make it a part of a shooting routine, which means on the clays course, reset the safety after each shot. It's simply the use of good common sense, and making the safety catch procedure a part of every shot could prevent an accident.

MAKING THE GUN SAFE DURING THE HUNT

When there are accidents during a hunt, they are often caused by the hunter's carelessness while crossing objects such as fences, creeks or rivers, rocks, and fallen trees. Such objects can force the hunter to make some unconventional moves with his feet and arms. As a result, when crossing such objects, it is proper to make the gun safe until the object has been safely crossed.

This is done by placing the gun and muzzle in a direction that renders it safe. When hunting with a partner, the gun(s) can be handed to the hunter who has crossed the object. This should be done with the muzzle placed in a safe position.

When hunting alone, the gun should be placed with the muzzle in a safe direction and out of the hands of the shooter until the object has been crossed. Once crossed, the gun can be retrieved by picking it up without touching the trigger.

If the object is of such a size that crossing it without the gun will make the gun unretrievable, the gun should be unloaded and the action rendered visibly open to be carried across the object.

There are more instances when crossing objects that guns have to be made safe. When getting in

It's best to lay your unloaded gun outside of the blind before you get in or out of your blind.

It is important for hunters to stay in line as they move through a field. Any hunter that gets too far ahead or behind should be repositioned for safety.

and out of blinds, especially blinds built at or below ground level, the guns should be unloaded and made safe as well. The same applies for stepping in and out of a boat.

Just to be on the safe side, it's a good idea to make the gun safe before you hand it to another person. This way there won't be a chance of a mistake.

ALWAYS BE AWARE OF YOUR SURROUNDINGS AND YOUR TARGET

It's pretty rare for bird hunters to hunt alone, so knowing where hunting partners and other hunters in the area are is a very important safety element. A shotgun can shoot a shot charge almost

1000 feet if some of the larger shot sizes are being used, and while it may not be lethal at that distance, the pellets can certainly cause damage to the eyes or other parts of the body if impacted properly.

At the distances that most hunters are from each other when hunting together for waterfowl or upland birds, a shotgun blast is lethal, so being aware of your fellow hunter's location is critical to the safety of the hunt. One way to insure safety is to map out a plan before the hunt actually begins. This simply means preplanning the positioning of each hunter in the field or blind, and establishing firing lanes for them. And since safety is everyone's responsibility, each hunter should be willing to point out and correct any potential safety problem he sees, no matter what the shooting venue is.

Firing lanes are very important, especially when hunters are walking an area where shots are expected to be taken. By walking parallel to each other, any shots taken will be downrange of the line of hunters, and as long as each shooter takes only birds in front of him, there should be no danger to other shooters in the line. Shots behind the line should be discouraged unless there is no question about the safety element involved in attempting such a shot. And such activity should be discussed and approved by all of the guns in the party.

It is obviously important to identify your target before shooting. Game bird laws often require hunters to shoot only certain species and often only the males of those species. So it makes sense to take the time to identify precisely what you are shooting at.

GUNS AND ALCOHOL JUST DON'T MIX

For generations bird hunting as been as much a social affair as it has a true hunting experience for most shooters. Unfortunately the social makeup of the sport can lead to alcohol consumption in some circles. Common sense will tell one that shooting and alcohol just don't mix, and any thoughts contrary to this are simply foolish. The belief that a sip of bourbon or brandy will help warm the body is pure myth, since alcohol has been proven to lower body temperatures rather than warm it. Any consumption of alcohol should take place after the hunt, and it's important that no one drive if impaired.

GUN SAFETY DOESN'T HAVE TO BE ROCKET SCIENCE

Good gun safety is simply a matter of paying attention to the details of handling the gun and being aware of one's surrounding. It's sort of like defensive driving in a car where problems are taken care of before they can happen. When safety becomes a priority for trips afield, chances are that good habits will develop and be passed down to all of the hunters in a particular group.

When it comes to gun safety, there is simply no compromise. We have been very fortunate in this country that so few accidents happen, but it only takes one careless act to change one's life permanently. So be safe and have fun.

You can extend the life of your favorite scattergun by performing a bit of gun maintenance in the field once the hunt ends. You will want to wipe the dirt, grime, fingerprints and sweat off of the outside of your gun before putting it in its case.

Shotgun Maintenance for the Field

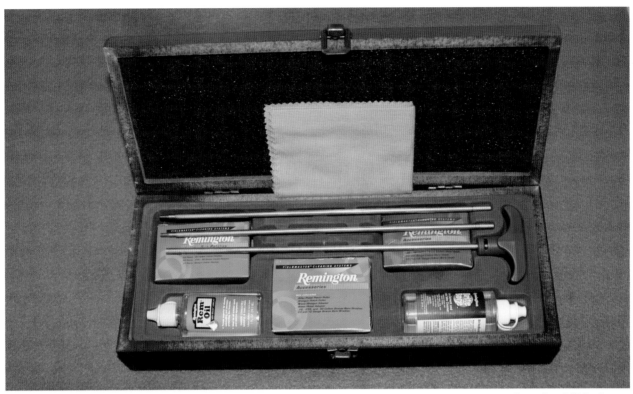

Most hunters do their thorough gun cleaning at home after the hunt. A good gun cleaning kit helps make the job easier.

Few things are more frustrating or unnerving to wingshooters than finding dirt, grime, rust spots or pits caused by improper shotgun maintenance following a day in the field. A dirty, unclean shotgun can malfunction at the least opportune time, and once rusting or pitting occurs in the metal its value can significantly diminish. Let's face it, when you pull the trigger, you expect your gun to fire. When it doesn't because it wasn't properly cleaned…well, that's your fault.

Most of the time a thorough cleaning job is better handled away from the field, but this doesn't mean that the gun should be simply thrown in a case once the hunt is over. There are a few things that can be done before the gun is stored for the trip from the field that will prolong its useful life and value.

In-the-field maintenance should include spraying the outside metal parts of the gun thoroughly with a good gun oil or protective lubricant and wiping it off with a dry cloth to remove any dirt or oily residue and salt left from handling the gun.

A good cleaning rod with an oiled cloth attached can help remove most of the powder residue, dirt and moisture from the interior of the barrel. The moisture can be present even in the driest of conditions because of the difference between temperatures that occurs when the barrel is quickly heated during firing and that of the surrounding air. This difference causes condensation to form in the chamber of the barrel, which in time will rust if not wiped dry.

These two field maintenance tips should be followed after every day afield, whether the gun is fired or not. It's better to be safe than sorry, and the process only takes a few minutes.

The main cleaning exercise, however, should take place once back at an overnight destination. Shooters can easily alleviate the possibility of malfunctions or devaluation of a firearm by taking a few steps to properly clean it following each use. These few simple cleaning methods mean that a gun will be ready for action when the urge to venture afield strikes again. It's best to establish a maintenance routine and stick by it.

It is important to have the right tools to properly clean your gun. Semiautomatic shotguns, especially the gas operated systems, tend to require more cleaning tools.

First of all, shooters should purchase a good gun cleaning kit or a combination of cleaning supplies. Items that are a must include bore solvent, a bore brush and chamber brush preferably made of brass, a quality gun oil, a toothbrush, cleaning rod, #4 steel wool and a soft, dry cloth. Each of these items play an important role in maintaining a shotgun properly.

When a gun is fired, unburned powder and other component residue is left in the bore. If left uncleaned, corrosion could occur over time, so it's a good idea to properly clean the bore every time the gun is used. Just running a cleaning rod through the barrel only partly does the job. A good bore solvent serves to break down any leftover component debris in the bore. Solvent is not really intended to serve as a lubricant, so once the bore has been cleaned a light coating of gun oil or protective lubricant should be added.

As the gun is shot, the chamber and barrel begin to heat up. The more quickly you shoot,

the hotter they get. When plastic hull loads are used, the heat can cause residue from the plastic to build up along chamber walls and plastic wad residue can build in the forcing cone. This can cause jamming in pump or semiautomatic action guns and rough chamber walls in double guns. A chamber brush will effectively remove any plas-

Tools like the Bore Snake can remove plastics deposits from hulls and wads that, over time, start to adhere to the bore and chamber of the gun.

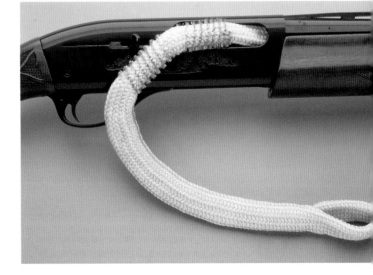

tic buildup and help insure that shells can be smoothly fed into the chamber.

A small wire brush should be used to clean plastic wad buildup and carbon residue at the mouth of the choke tube. This buildup can cause inconsistent pattern performance if left unchecked. Immersing the choke, if it can be removed, in bore solvent will loosen this residue and make cleaning easier.

Once the choke tube has been removed, be sure to clean the threads with a brush before screwing the choke back into the gun. A light coat of oil

If you're going to clean your gun, then clean it. Take it down as completely as possible so you can properly clean all of the parts.

will protect the threads and make choke changing much easier. Over and under or double guns can be maintained with less work than guns with pump or semiautomatic actions. The main reason for this is the difference in the number of moving parts in each of the actions.

In addition to the barrel cleaning, the receivers on gun actions need to be cleaned as well. Bore solvent, a toothbrush or piece of steel wool and a soft wiping cloth will get into crevices where dirt and residue can collect. These items will remove any carbon buildup that has gathered around the firing pins as well. Be sure that once the receiver is clean, you add a light coat of oil to protect the gun and so that the metal to metal parts work smoothly.

Semiautomatic and pump action guns require a bit more work to properly maintain them. The auto action models, especially those with gas operated systems, should be disassembled after every use, because the nature of the action has a tendency to leave excess residue on its moving parts. The small gas ports in the barrel should be periodically cleaned with a piercing object like a pipe cleaner to remove carbon buildup clogging the holes. At the same time, the magazine tube and the ejection slide tube that moves over it should be wiped clean as well. Failure to do this will cause the gun to jam at some point.

Some gas operated guns seem to work better when sprayed with a lubricant, while others are better shot dry. For instance, the Beretta gas operated autos are more efficient when the outside of the magazine tube is sprayed lightly with a lubricating agent. On the other hand, the Remington 1100 and 11-87 seem to function better when their magazine tubes are sprayed with a lubricant and then wiped off, leaving just a film coat of the lubricating agent.

Pump actions are similar in operation to some autos, and should be disassembled and cleaned much the same way. Since the action is operated by physical force, a light coat of lubricant on the moving parts of the gun will ease shell ejection and chamber loading, and will serve to protect the moving parts against the elements and wear.

Regardless of the gun action, if the trigger assembly has been exposed to extreme moisture or firing, it's best to remove it to properly clean and dry it. With double guns, the trigger is usually exposed by removing the stock. In some instances, triggers are removable with the push of a button,

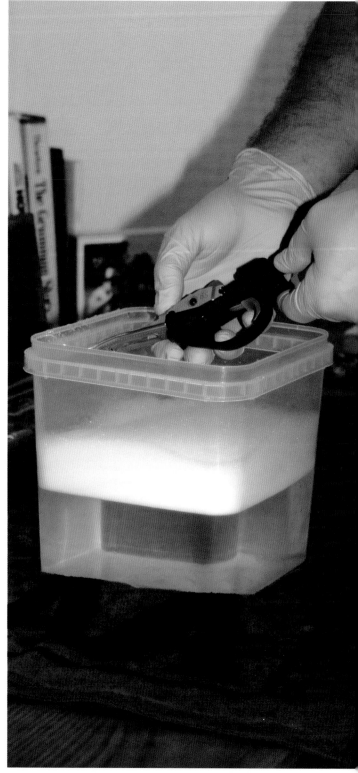

One of the best ways to clean a trigger assembly is to submerge and clean it in hot, soapy water. The hot water and soap will break a lot of grit and powder residue away from the trigger assembly. Make sure it is dry and lubricated before putting it back in the gun.

which allows the trigger to release and be pulled away from the receiver. In most autos and pumps, the trigger assembly can be removed by knocking out a couple of support pins.

Most shooters will be amazed at how much dirt and unburned powder is collected by the trigger assembly when the gun is fired. This can be removed by some type of commercial gun scrubber or gun solvent and a soft brush. It can also be cleaned with hot soapy water which breaks down the oil or grease that has accumulated over time. Once the trigger assembly has been allowed to dry, a light coat of gun oil or lubricant should be added before it is put back into the gun.

Once the internal working parts of the gun have been cleaned and lubricated, it can be either reassembled for use or prepared for storage. The external metal parts should be sprayed with some protective lubricant and wiped with a dry cloth.

Use the toothbrush or pipe cleaners to remove dirt and debris from under the sections of vented ribs.

Wood components of the gun such as the stock and forearm should also be protected. Some shooters like to use a mild furniture polish or wood cleaner to restore the luster to satin or high gloss finished woods. A lightly oiled cloth can be used on oil treated or finished woods.

Proper gun maintenance is not time consuming. So take the time to wipe your gun off before leaving the field, and give it a thorough cleaning before storing it for the day. By taking these easy steps, you will help insure both its value and operation for years to come.

It is important to clean under the rib of your shotgun to prevent corrosion from forming. Q-tips and pipe cleaners work great along with some good gun oil.

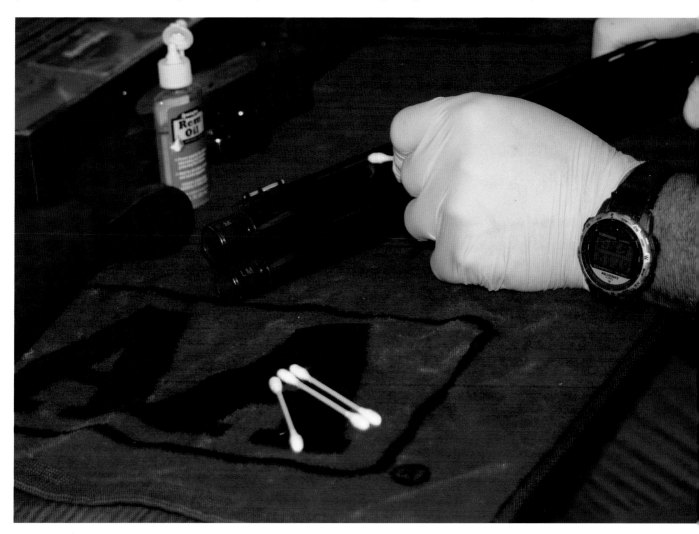

Practicing With a Purpose

No matter how much you get to hunt these days, game bird limits just don't let you develop your wingshooting skills properly if the only shooting you do is while hunting. Simply put, for you to be the best you can be, you have to practice away from the field and on a year round basis. Let's take a look at some of the various ways you can practice with a purpose.

Some forms of practice cost nothing but a bit of time, but they can be very effective. Gun mount practice and eye exercises are two of the best things a shooter can do year round. And since gun mount mechanics and vision are two of the most important elements of a shot, they can really help your game.

CLAYS, CLAYS AND MORE CLAYS

Clay target shooting in America got its start in the late 1800s. Cincinnati native George Ligowski invented the clay pigeon. The clay pigeon and subsequently the game of trap took the place of live pigeon shooting. In the 1920s the game of

Once sporting clays came to American shores, new guns, more functional shooting glasses and custom digital hearing protection became the norm for clay enthusiasts. Fortunately these products have found their way into the hands of many wingshooters.

skeet was developed in order to give wingshooters a way to practice different shot angles they might encounter in the field. In the 1980s, sporting clays came to America from England, and in just a few years it has become the most popular clay target game for hunters. All three of these games are quite popular in many regions of the world, especially America.

Many hunters tend to shy away from visiting clay target clubs and ranges because they feel somewhat intimidated by a perception that gun clubs are only for competitive shooters. Nothing can be further from the truth. Fact is the vast majority of clay target shooters aren't intense competitive types at all. Most are either hunters or recreational shooters who enjoy shooting. They

(above) There is a competitive element to clay target shooting if you want to participate.

(below) Many clay targets are not shot at gun clubs at all. They are shot by friends on private property near their homes.

are far from being professional shooters.

Does that competitive element exist? Of course it does, just like it does in golf, tennis or any other sport for that matter. But only a very small percentage of shooters are classified as pros, so most of them are just like you, and there's no reason for you to stay away.

If you've got a sporting clays facility in your area, it might be wise for you to spend some time there. A good clays range can offer more shot variety over the course of a hundred or so targets than one could set up in an entire day. If all that's available at a local gun club is trap or skeet, spend some time there as well. Keep in mind, however, that if one's goals are to improve hunting skills, it's not necessary to get caught up in premounting the gun prior to taking a shot like the competition guys do. It's better to make sure that things are put into proper perspective, including score. You see, when skill development is a goal, keeping score should be discouraged. You can bet that the better scores will come as you learn to play the game properly.

Without question, the vast majority of clay target shooting takes place away from any organized shooting range. For the most part, shooters practice with groups of their friends using either hand traps or inexpensive mechanical throwers in a field or safe location near their homes. Each year millions and millions of rounds of ammo are fired at clays thrown at virtually every imaginable speed, angle and distance. Unfortunately, many shooters really don't have an idea of how to present clay pigeons to best develop their shotgun skills. If you have a proper place to practice this way, here are a couple of pointers that will help make those efforts more fruitful.

First of all, the most important aspect of any practice is safety. So regardless of the type of practicing that is planned, special care should be taken to insure the safety of all persons involved. Try setting up a vertical pole or post to serve as a stop for the gun. This will insure that the gun can't be pointed in the direction of the trap, and it will prohibit the shooter from turning in the direction of others. Two gun stops positioned 48 inches apart will give you the same effect as shooting stations on a clays course. Of course you can also make an inexpensive and lightweight shooting station out of PVC.

Because wingshooters are safety conscious, they spend much of their time with the trap near their side, blasting at clays thrown away from them, much like regulation trap targets. These types of birds are fine if the majority of their shooting is at flushing birds such as quail, pheasant, grouse, etc. But since most shooters seem to have problems hitting high driven or crossing shots in the field, the only way to improve one's skills on those types of shots is to practice them.

As mentioned earlier, the types of shot presentations that can by set up safely is virtually limitless, so identifying your weak points in the field and then duplicating them with clays really isn't that difficult. There are ways to set up a mini sporting clays course using just one manual trap, and here's how to do it.

Start with the straight away target by releasing a target or series of targets from your side. Keep in mind that speed and elevation changes can be made to even the most economical of manual traps, so these changes can be made from time to time, too.

Since safety is of paramount importance when shooting in an informal setting, establishing gun stops with some kind of vertical pole is a smart thing.

You can build your own shooting stand out of PVC for little money. Use a four foot by four foot base with a front rail 34 inches from the ground and gun stops in front that are 84 inches from the ground.

If you are a dove hunter, you will want to work on driven or crossing targets.

Move shooting positions either to the right or left a few feet, and the shot presentation will completely change the shot angle taken at the previous stand. As a shooting position is moved, the target presentation will constantly change because the angle of that presentation is changing too. The major concern when setting up or moving either the shooter or the trap is the safety of the person operating the trap and the down range shot fall area that needs to be considered for safety's sake.

When using manual traps, a protective barrier should be used anytime the trap is positioned in front of the shooter. This barrier should be portable so that it can move if there is ever a reason to move the trap. The barrier should be constructed of either wood or metal that cannot be pierced by shot should an unlikely accident occur. Some

Many shooters own a personal manual trap. Of course the manual thrower requires that you have at least one friend to shoot with.

shooters utilize large round hay bales as barriers. These are certainly acceptable as long as the trap and trapper are completely obscured from the shooter. Multiple bales are better because of their size. When using a manual trap and barrier, make sure to include a safety flag to signal that a trapper is manning the machine.

By utilizing a single trap and barrier, shooters have the flexibility to shift their positions so as to create a wide variety of shots that might be taken in the field. When this happens, the chances of developing solid field skills are greatly enhanced.

You will find that by using an automatic thrower a wide variety of shooting angles is possible without the need for a protective barrier. You might want to protect the trap, so a cover of some kind can be easily added. There are a number personal automatic clay target traps on the market today. Many are easily affordable, especially if you and your friends collectively make the purchase. Keep in mind, too, that that the more traps you have available, the more different angles and speeds you can throw.

If this type of shooting opportunity doesn't exist in your particular area, or if a change of pace is required for practice, try visiting a local trap, skeet or sporting clays range. These ranges will provide hours of fun and excitement, and can provide additional variety for shot selection.

A hunter who has no real interest in becoming a competitive clay shooter should try shooting all of these games with the gun in the off shoulder position before calling for the target. You won't have the gun premounted on the shoulder when in the field, so shouldering it before calling for a target in these games won't offer you any help with gun mount either.

Keep in mind that good shooting starts with good mechanics, and being able to consistently shoulder the gun in the same place is a major piece of the overall puzzle. It should also be noted that if a shooter is constantly having trouble hitting a particular clay, it's all right to shoulder the gun to get the right line and lead picture. Once the forward allowance required for a shot is found, it's best to try to make the shot consistently from the low gun position.

PRACTICE FOR THE BEGINNER TO NOVICE SHOOTER

One of the most discouraging things a new shooter faces is the prospect of not being able to hit anything. This is especially true for youth and ladies shooters. We must keep in mind that when introducing someone to wingshooting, the initial experience has to be enjoyable if they are expected to want to do it again.

As alluded to in earlier chapters, low recoil ammo fired from properly fitted guns with open chokes all mean early success and extended enjoyment. All too often, dad hands junior his heavy, tight choked 12 bore stuffed with magnum loads for that first experience. Not only is this the wrong approach, it could spell disaster for the newcomer's shooting future.

Sporting clays is not just for the guys. There are lots of ladies and kids on clay courses these days.

If there is any fly in the ointment of the sporting clays shooter, it is that the game now has a free mount rule. In other words, if the shooter wants to premount the gun before calling for the target, he is free to do so. Don't try that in the field when hunting birds. Fact is that in many instances, a premounted gun is a detriment to a sporting clays shooter.

The other end of this spectrum is to hand that same new shooter a .410 bore, sensing that the light recoil will make the gun more pleasurable to shoot, which would make it easier for the newbie to hit his target. If all the novice shooter is doing is shooting a stationary target with the little gun, that's fine. But putting a new shooter in a situation where he is asked to shoot a moving target with such a small shotgun won't be much a of confidence builder in most cases. Remember that the .410 is a scattergun more suited for the hands of professionals than for novices when it comes to shooting moving targets. The low recoil is not a fair tradeoff for the low pellet count and narrow, long shot string of this gauge. In reality, the newcomer would be far better off both on clays and birds if he started on either a 20 or 28 bore, or even a 12 gauge with low recoil training loads. At least the chances of early success are within reach to even the most novice of shooters.

Most of the time it's best to start a new shooter with the gun premounted on the shoulder. This will eliminate the requirements of a consistent gun mount and allow the shooter to simply concentrate on the target, the lead picture and his swing and follow through. Remember, the gun mount is a learned and practiced series of movements, and should be added to the overall shot sequence once it becomes comfortable.

When starting a new shooter or when working out a problem shot, there are three basic targets that professional instructors use to introduce newcomers to wingshooting, or to fix problems before they become habits. The fortunate thing for a shooter to know is that he, too, can easily set up those presentations, and go back to them when troubles arise with a particular shot.

In no particular order, the three basic shots are: straight away, slow crosser and incomer. Consider that many of the shots taken in the field fall into these categories, so learning to shoot them successfully will surely improve one's efficiency on real birds.

Both the experienced gun and the novice can significantly benefit from periodic workouts on these types of shots. They tend to serve a number of purposes for the basic training needed to

(above) The most basic of all shot presentations is the straight away target. This is a great starter target for the new shooter. It teaches the novice to focus on the target and take the gun to it to break it.

(left) The slow crosser is another of the basic presentations on a clays course. This type of shot helps teach the new shooter that sometimes you have to miss the target ahead in order to hit it.

become proficient on birds. Any of these types of targets can be demanding to some shooters, but each of them requires the same basic fundamentals that are required any time you shoot at a flying object or bird with a shotgun regardless of its speed, angle or distance.

One thing is certain when it comes to shooting the basic targets when shooting clays: If you can't hit them consistently, chances are that live birds presenting themselves in a similar manner in the field won't be hit either. So work diligently on the basic shots at a range of 20 to 25 yards at first.

The long incoming target is the third of the basic clay presentations that new shooters need to learn to shoot. These types of targets teach patience, and allow the newby to work on his gun mount and insertion points.

Don't think that shooting targets at fairly close ranges makes them easy. Remember that good shooting matches target pace with the shooter's pace, and that live birds will present themselves at a variety of speeds, angles and distances, including close in. Once you have mastered a shot, make sure you've got a mental picture of what picture hits it. Then you can simply change the trap setting to encounter another challenge.

Remember that there are but a handful of reasons why a bird is missed, and going back to the basics when encountering a problem will usually guarantee future success. The amount of time spent practicing gun mounts will transfer directly to the practice range and then to the field, and

A skeet field is a great place to practice your wingshooting, especially if you practice with the gun starting off the shoulder. Many clubs give you the freedom to back away from the shooting pads a bit, which will increase the distance to the target. The game of skeet was designed to give shooters a wide array of shot angles.

making sure that foot and body positioning allows a proper mount, swing, and follow through as the shot is taken will mean more kills than misses.

WORKING BACK TO THE BASICS

Since there should be a purpose for all practice, understanding how to deal with a problem is the key to solving it. Let's assume that a shooter has had good success with quartering birds both in the field and with clays. One day, however, he finds himself struggling to kill the quartering shot. What's wrong? Here's where the benefit of the basics comes into play.

Assuming a comfortable foot and body position for the shot and a good initial muzzle location and mount, what can be done to work out the problem? The simplest way to work on a problem or

One of the best things you can do for your shooting is find a competent shooting instructor. The right coach can make small changes that will instantly improve your skills in the field.

hard shot is to make it easier to hit. This is done by turning the presentation into one of the basic presentations. In the case of the quartering bird, change the shooting position to make it more of a straight away target. Once that shot has been taken a few times comfortably, move part of the way toward the troublesome quartering location. After success there, chances are moving back to the original spot where the trouble began will be easier yet. Keep in mind that in most instances, the difference between hitting and missing a bird will be fractions of an inch when looking down and beyond the muzzle of the gun.

If a troublesome bird is presented as a crosser, moving to a more quartering angle where the required lead is diminished will provide a foundation to work from. Again, find success and work slowly back to the problem shot. Once the right lead picture is found though, it's best to break it a couple of times and come back to it early in the next practice session to see if the sight picture was retained.

WHEN ALL ELSE FAILS, GET SOME HELP

For whatever reason, people will seek help in order to improve at just about any game they play except shooting. Golfers readily sign up for lessons in order to improve their game. Professional athletes in virtually every sport have coaches to help them work on problems in their respective games, but the shooting sports are far behind the curve when it comes to shooting instruction.

The popularity of sporting clays in America has seen a shift in this trend in recent years, but shooters in this country pale in numbers taking shooting lessons when compared to their European and UK counterparts. Shooting schools can be found at just about every shooting facility there, while for years, American shooters had to travel great distances for quality instruction. At many gun clubs stateside, the only help you could get was from some of the better shooters there. Unfortunately those good shooters are not necessarily trained to teach shooting properly.

Fortunately, you can probably find quality instruction within a short drive of where you live if you look for it. These days, there are numerous websites such as www.nssf.org and www.mynsca.com

Some instructors work one on one, but in many instances you will get more from a group lesson at first. This will give you rest and a chance to listen to what other shooters might be doing in success and failure.

that list clubs and instructors in your area.

When locating an instructor, make sure you let him know exactly what you are looking for. Many instructors will focus on teaching you to shoot only clays and not birds. You can learn to shoot birds by shooting clays, but there are subtle differences in the two.

Birds tend to take off slowly and speed up or maintain their pace as they fly. Clay targets from a trap take off at full speed and begin to slow down once they encounter the atmosphere. As a result, there are differences that must be dealt with when teaching wingshooting using clay targets.

Target setters have the ability to set their targets to replicate birds in flight at the time they are going to be shot. A good wingshooting instructor will create a hunting situation by having his student work on gun mounts and taking the targets with the proper aggressiveness for the shot at hand. If the student's interest is in shooting long passing shots or decoying birds, the instructor will modify his lesson and your style so that shooting those presentations is comfortable. If your interest is in shooting flushing or driven birds, the instructor will introduce you to targets that best fit those types of shots. He will also work with your default shooting style in order to mold it to comfortably fit those types of shots. The good news is that he can do all of this using clay targets.

The major advantage to finding the right shooting instructor is that he can build you as a shooter over time. Rest assured, great wingshots are not developed in a day, just as Rome wasn't built in a day. It will take time, but the right instructor can help you significantly shorten the learning curve.

PROPER PRACTICE PREVENTS POOR PERFORMANCE

There is no question that being able to practice properly helps us improve in every endeavor we pursue. And since having the opportunity to

The high dove tower shots give shooters fits. This particular tower shot was designed by the author for the Oshawa Trap and Skeet Club in Canada.

Shooters on a clay course are usually at different levels with their game. Wingshooters can learn to apply techniques learned on a clays course to shots taken while hunting.

practice shooting skills on live birds is generally prohibitive, getting out to a trap, skeet or sporting clays range or just shooting a few clays with your friends will open the door to increased success. Just remember that every shooting session should serve to improve one's wingshooting skills. Set a goal for shooting practice, and don't worry about keeping score. When practicing with a purpose, shooters are certain to realize the fruits of their labors in the field.

For instance, if your goal is to work on crossing shots, start on shots that you feel comfortable with. Work diligently on your consistency by making your insertion points as perfect as possible. The goal should be to develop this consistency to where it is almost automatic.

If you are struggling after a dozen or so shots, walk away from it and come back. If you have the freedom to do so, move your shooting location to

You get a completely different perspective of targets and birds when your eyes are positioned lower to the ground. The goose pit shot at Birds Landing Hunting Preserve in California has been frustrating shooters for more than a decade.

make the target more comfortable to shoot. Then work your way back to your starting spot. If you hit it a couple of times, go somewhere else. You can stay in one spot too long, and it will only create bad habits.

When a shooter has the perfect stance, mount, insertion point, lead picture and follow through, the result is a harvested bird. This pigeon in Argentina was moving left to right. Note the shooter's head still in the gun and the feather trail to the left of the bird.

Putting It All Together

Some of the best duck hunting in the world is found in the Santa Fe province of Argentina. These ducks were taken in one afternoon on a hunt with SYC Sporting Adventures.

As we have seen, good wingshooting technique and mechanics can be learned and practiced away from the field, but only when you strive to put all of the pieces together will your skills begin to match your expectations. Keep in mind that before golfer Tiger Woods won his first Masters title, he had honed and practiced his skills for many, many years. And after he won the event, he decided to make a number of changes to his game that would make him even better. The very best wingshooters, too, have developed their skills with years of practice and experience, and the savvy ones know that they can find ways to be even better in the field.

Without question, new shooters have a tendency to expect too much, too soon. Perhaps this is merely human nature. We often desperately desire a level of perfection without working for it. After all, an acceptable level of success is every shooter's goal. Unfortunately that level of expectation is completely different from person to person, so let's get real, and go over our plan to shooting utopia.

Let's recap the measures for success in wing-

shooting by starting at the top. Get a gun that fits you properly, and learn to mount and swing it so that those movements become second nature. Make it a point to practice your gun mounts during the off season, and there's no better way to do that than by shooting a few rounds of clays starting well before opening day. You should shoot as much as you desire or at least as much as your time constraints and budget will allow. If you can shoot year round, do so. And if your budget has room for a bit of shooting instruction, take it.

Take the time to learn as much as possible about the birds you will be hunting. Building a knowledge base of what makes a game bird tick is a major part of being prepared for a shot when it comes. Many hunters find that acquiring knowledge about the game they hunt is often as exciting and fulfilling as the hunting experience itself.

You can never forget the importance of a good insertion point when it comes to your wingshooting. If you get sloppy and miss it, there's a good chance that you will miss.

When choosing a gun for a particular hunt, make sure you know what choke and load combination will give you the best chances for success. Let's not forget that 60 percent of wingshooting is confidence, and knowing the performance characteristics of your equipment is a real confidence builder.

Work diligently on technique and get comfortable with more than one of the prescribed shooting styles. By having a few more tools in your

shooting tool box, you will take major strides towards that consistent success in the field you are looking for. And keep in mind that regardless of which style is chosen, matching your pace with that of the target initially will help get the gun in position for a successful shot.

Make concentration and focus an integral part of every shot. Remember how important target focus is for every shot, because if the eyes aren't looking at the target there's a very good chance that the gun isn't either. And since we haven't yet developed feather-seeking lead shot, placing a shot charge other than in the right place relative to the bird will result in a miss.

Hunters will find that focusing on the front or leading edge of the bird will give them an advantage when it comes to getting the gun in front of a speeding target. They would be wise to concentrate on the bird's head if it is quartering, crossing or rising, and get a good handle on the line of flight that it is taking. With birds landing straight in to the shooter, looking more at the feet of the bird will help position it properly under the bird.

Some clay shooters imagine there is a clock face around the bird so they can come to the line of flight easier. For instance, if a flushed bird is rising at a quartering right angle, the leading edge or head of the target is moving to approximately 2:00 on the clock face. By focusing on the head of the bird, the hands will move the bird to the 2:00 position, which will make it much easier to move the gun to the front of the target.

Remember that perfecting things like concentration, focus and practice are designed for one thing...to give you the confidence to make a shot regardless of the speed, angle or distance of the bird. And it is this confidence level that will make you the accomplished wingshooter that you strive so hard to be. You can bet that as your consistency improves, the hard work you continue to put into your game will be well worth the time and effort.

Once you have a handle, so to speak, on the visual, mechanical and mental aspects of wingshooting, you will continue to improve by sticking to your basic fundamentals. Every time you harvest a bird with a particular shooting style, you will add a little more to your mental library of shots. Let's take one last look at the various types of shot presentations you might encounter afield and list a few pointers that will make shooting such presentations more instinctive.

FLUSHING BIRDS

When it comes to wingshooting, perhaps more birds of the flushing variety are shot worldwide each year than any other type. The game bird species that offer such shot presentations include all of the upland species, as well as flushing waterfowl.

In most shot scenarios the flushing target is probably the least complex of all shot types because there is usually less gun movement and lead required to make a successful shot. The vast majority of flushing shots are of the straight away or quartering variety. These shallow angle presentations usually afford the shooter more time to act than he might think. A typical shot analysis will take you through the steps to success.

Let's break the flushing shot down frame by frame. When moving in on a bird that will present a flushing shot, you should be totally aware of your surroundings. Where are the trees, the dogs, the possible shot windows and other obstacles where the gun should not be pointed? Most impor-

Since most hunters can tell time, using a clock-face to determine direction, visual focus and insertion point locations makes sense.

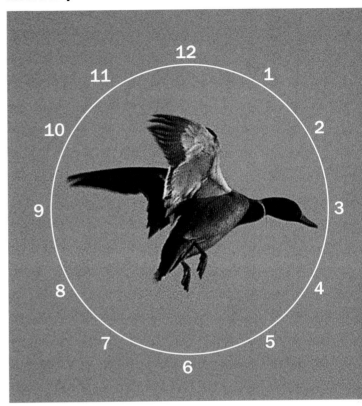

tantly, where are the other hunters in your party? Once those things are identified before the flush, the shot sequence can begin. If you are constantly

Once birds flush in mass, you've got to quickly read the presentation angle. Most birds will still be in range once you determine the direction the bird is traveling.

Remember that when targets are presented in a more vertical fashion, things like hand position and balance are very important.

least amount of movement possible. With a rush of wings the bird flushes. For the new shooter, all hell breaks loose. For the experienced gun, the eyes go to the target and lock focus on it to slow it down visually. Once the target focus is obtained, the hands and gun have a direction of where to steer the muzzle. As this is taking place, you make a subtle move with your front foot by stepping towards your shot window. If you do it right, you will have all the grace and beauty of a ballet dancer.

Your focus has allowed you to identify your target, its speed, angle of presentation and its distance. In one smooth motion you are able to bring the muzzle of the gun just behind or on the bird and the stock of the gun to your face.

Since you have read the angle of presentation, you will instinctively know whether or not you need to lead the bird. With the visual focus on the target and through the gun, you can move the muzzle relative to the bird until your eyes tell the brain that the picture looks right. At that moment the trigger is pulled, but the gun continues to move with the bird. The eyes stay focused on the target and watch the bird fall thorough the beads of the gun.

Sounds simple doesn't it? It certainly can be when there's no rushing and no stress. We have identified how to make this shot sequence happen. When all of the pieces do come together correctly, such a shot seems effortless.

DRIVEN BIRDS

The overhead bird that is coming towards your shooting position can be identified as driven. Such shots are common when hunting doves and waterfowl, and while blocking for pheasants or other birds being pushed in your direction.

The driven target coming towards the shooter can be defined as a crossing target, but the technique to hit such a bird is somewhat different from the traditional crossing bird. Since the shot angle is changing from a low angle to a more vertical shot, the hand position on the gun and weight transfer to move it through the shot sequence tend to be different from a crossing bird with a lower trajectory. Both the crossing bird and the incom-

moving with flushing dogs, you must update this information continuously.

As you move to the shot, your muzzle is positioned in such a way that you can focus on your target and move the muzzle into position with the

Decoying birds can be easy to hit as long as they don't start changing direction and speed. Once that happens, the technique to shoot them changes quickly.

This bird was landing seconds before this shot was taken. In wingshooting, those changes can take place quickly, and the best wingshooters can rapidly adjust to those changes of speed, angle and distance.

ing driven bird are presented 90 degrees to the shooter, but the elevation of the target is quite different.

When shooting an incoming driven bird, it is very important to establish the proper line of the bird. Most shooters do this by inserting the muzzle of the gun just behind the target and pulling through the head of the bird. The visual focus is on the leading edge or head of the bird because this type of shot does, in fact, require some lead to hit.

Strangely enough, all of the recognized shooting styles can be applied to this type of target. Which style is most comfortable would be determined primarily by the distance and speed of the bird, since the faster and farther the shot is, the more lead you would need to hit it. The presentation angle for a driven shot is predictable. The target speed and distance is not. The best style for a driven

shot is the one where the gun moves smoothly through the line of the bird and to the proper lead.

Many shooters make the mistake of waiting too long before starting the shot sequence on driven birds. On the other hand, some start the gun too quickly. Let's analyze the shot.

On high driven birds, the gun must move with the bird. As it moves, the shooter's weight starts on the front foot and transfers to the back foot as the bird flies overhead. The forearm hand can be positioned slightly closer to the receiver of the gun since once the bird is straight overhead, the shooter will be fully extended.

The style for low driven birds is somewhat different because the shooter will want to take his first shot well in front of his position. This will give him the chance to take subsequent shots more comfortably. The lower angle will not re-

quire as much lead since the presentation at the lower heights will be less than 90 degrees. The closer the birds get to the gun, the more lead will be required to harvest it. Once again, the weight transfer is from the front foot to the back foot as the bird moves toward the gun.

DECOYING BIRDS

Most of the birds we hunt are either maintaining or increasing speed when we take a shot, but when shooting decoying birds, the target is slowing down as it attempts to land. Once the bird senses your movement, it changes its angle and speed as quickly as possible. These speed changes cause you to change the pace of your approach and follow through to the shot.

Perhaps the most important aspect of shooting a decoying target is to not rush the gun. Simply

move as the bird moves and then bring the gun into the target as it moves. As this takes place, keep the gun moving forward of the line of the bird until the lead feels right. Remember that the speed of the target dictates the initial speed of the gun. As the lead picture develops the trigger can be squeezed. Make sure to keep the gun moving for the follow through, and by all means keep the head down and through the beads of the gun until you see the bird fall. Since the presentation angle starts to change quickly once your presence is detected, the bird can be shot as either a flushing or crossing target.

CROSSING BIRDS

It has been established earlier that the most difficult shot for most wingshooters is the crossing target. In a crossing scenario the bird presents itself at or near 90 degrees to the shooter. This presentation angle requires the most forward allowance of any bird being shot at that same distance and speed. The complexity of this shot lies in the crossing angle.

Crossing shots take so much lead for a successful shot, shooting styles that actually place the gun in front of the bird tend to work best. Since lead pictures should be felt and not measured, you must trust your eyes to tell you when the forward lead is right. When the picture looks right, you must have the guts to pull the trigger and keep the gun moving.

When shooting crossing targets, you usually have time to visually acquire the target. Once again a leading edge focus will help with the insertion point and the line of the bird. The more precise your focus, the more finite you can be in the shot sequence.

As the target is sighted, make a subtle move to set your feet just before initiating the shot sequence. With the bird in focus, begin moving the

Things like muzzle pace and insertion points are critical when it comes to crossing birds. The long crossing bird can be the most difficult of shots for many hunters, but once you've got the technique down, making such shots is not so difficult.

body and gun with the bird. This speed is essentially the same as the bird. As you move with the bird and focus on it, the gun comes to the face at the intended insertion point.

The insertion point should be at a position relative to the bird so that you can execute the shooting style you think will be most comfortable. Most of the shooters who shoot crossing birds well don't look out of control. If you have too much gun speed, you will usually miss the bird.

Once again the eyes will let the brain know when the picture looks right. If the gun continues to move when that picture is identified, a successful shot should be the result. Keep in mind that shooting crossing targets is much like throwing a football to a receiver crossing in front of you. You must throw the ball in front of him if you want him to catch the ball without changing pace. The same principal applies when shooting a crossing bird.

As you can see, mastering these different shots doesn't require you to be off pace with the bird. In most cases, if you do what the bird does and a little bit more, you've got a great chance for a successful shot. And after all, that is what the shot phase of the wingshooting experience is all about.

When hunting, shooters should constantly scan the sky for birds. Once a bird is spotted, moving the gun to the insertion point, feeling the lead move forward and keeping the head in the gun through the follow through will insure a successful shot.

EPILOGUE

What is it about a beautiful flock of Northern mallards slip sliding into a decoy set that makes the heart of every waterfowler race? And what makes the upland gunner marvel at the splendor of the flush of the magnificent cock pheasant, or the skyward explosion of a bevy of bobwhites from under the nose of an English pointer standing rock hard on point? Such experiences have been described as pictures that no artist could paint. For the true sportsman, they are the essence of the why he hunts.

For the wingshooting purist, the actual shooting portion of a day afield is dwarfed by the overall experience. For the true hunter, simply the opportunity to be there is reward enough. For those of us who live to watch our breath wisped away across the cattails on a cold morning, or sense the bond between man and dog when a job has been well done, a certain respect is owed to the upland birds and waterfowl we hunt. In the mind of a true sportsman, it's an honor and privilege to enter their world.

In a nutshell, that's what this book has been about. It was written to give you more insight into how to get more enjoyment from a day in the field and to help you become a better wingshooter by virtue of increased knowledge.

As this is being written, I'm on a Delta jet heading westward to gun whitewings just South of the Mexican border. The decisions I make regarding which shots to take, the chokes to use and which style will work for each individual shot will have already been made before the gun ever comes to my cheek for the first time. Years of experience have given me a confidence level that when my eyes focus beyond the rib to a chosen speeding bird, I expect to make a successful shot when the trigger is pulled. Hopefully after reading the many thousands of words in this book, you too will have a better understanding of what it takes to reach that same level of confidence when shooting afield.

There are few things that could give me more pleasure than penning these words. Perhaps a hot cup of coffee shared with friends one crisp fall morning while watching skeins of waterfowl overhead would do it. Or maybe a brisk walk with a favorite hunting partner watching a brace of well-trained pointers at work, or my new Lab pup busily nosing native grasses for one whiff of a wily rooster. Perhaps we'll meet afield one day. If that meeting is not here on earth, maybe then in wingshooting heaven. If you love the outdoors as I do, you can bet that just being there in good company will help make the experience as good as it can get.

Be safe, good shooting and by all means give the outdoors the respect it deserves.

The Shooter's Library

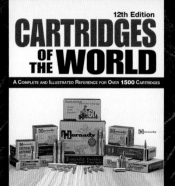
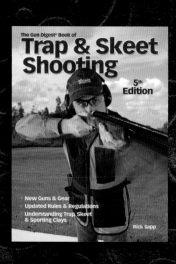
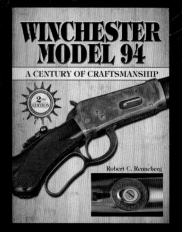